LEADERSHIP:
Where Business Ethics Begin

Student's Edition

LEADERSHIP:
Where Business Ethics Begin

Student's Edition

Thomas F. Franklin

Edited by Jody Serey

Franklin Leadership, Inc.

Table of Contents

Foreword

*Definitions, page 153

**Bibliography, page 193

***Root ideas, page 144

It is my belief that it is easy to make business theory and practice difficult, and it is difficult to make it easy. I have found this to be true over the last 30 years by working with managers, senior executives, presidents and chief executive officers as they tried to develop their mission, culture, and operating statements.

Before it became an acceptable leadership objective to integrate comprehensive marketing, financial and management decisions together in a strategic management process, I was crafting such ideas and words on a blank page. The result was a series of statements that dealt with disparate parts* of a company. For example, statements on strategic marketing, financial targets and management processes

1

found within the strategic management schematic pages 56 and 57 would be developed. These would be used to impact everyone and their understanding of their roles in the creation of value*. This would be accomplished not only for themselves, but for their customers and clients as they communicated the ideas to them.

I began my focus and love of business theory before I attended my first formal business class. I was 12 years old, sitting on my porch folding newspapers and the question surfaced in my mind, "Why are people willing to pay me all this money, $3.50 a week, to deliver 45 papers six days a week?"

After thinking about that question and trying to understand what motivated adults, I came to the conclusion that if I were a working adult it would be important to have all the newest daily information available before I went to work. I also realized that the earlier the working adult had the paper (a dry paper was also easier to read), then people could read it before and during their train commute to work.

I knew I was hooked on business as a vocation when I was finishing my undergraduate studies. As I walked by the new psychology and sociology buildings, a thought came to me about all of us students in the 60s who wanted to save the world. The unknown inevitability was that we would all become part of the only organization that would create change for everyone, the business entity. Whether we realized it or not, it was the many different types of business organizations that would change the face of our future. This activity of creating change, whether it is realized or not, is a root cause* of why a business entity exists.

It is pure and simple. The only organizations whose primary purpose is to take the physical elements and create something of value for people are the differing types of business entities. A simple example that we all but take for granted is that of creating a plastic pen to record our ideas which requires an understanding of how to process oil into plastic material and then forming it into a writing stick.

The challenge of this book is to make understandable these very abstract ideas and concepts that are responsible for the above physicalization process *. This is especially true if you are looking to evolve your own leadership philosophy — something that is so subtle that we do not realize that we live with that philosophy every moment of our lives. It determines our quality of life as we move through our career and life cycles.

In addition, just as the physical world moves through cycles, so do the cycles of excellence and non-excellence within both individuals and companies. These cycles also determine the level and success of these companies and individuals by manifesting both hard dollar* and soft dollar * results.

Managing physical cycles effectively will be a result of new leadership vision. Awareness, ability and focus will result in the cessation of judging leadership in absolute terms of weak or strong. This will be important because within the process of judging, objectivity and insight becomes lost by individuals. In addition, the issues being judged are the root cause* of where the leader can end up wasting time on the wrong issues. The result is leaders reaching conclusions that can be 180 degrees off.

One of the most important results within this new millennium will be the understanding of the cyclical nature of value creation. This should result in a significant decrease in the amount of time and effort spent by CEOs and leaders trying to straighten out hard dollar results from natural cycles of value creation. This refocus away from a short term performance should have the effect of simplifying the monthly, quarterly and annual financial reporting activity. This new understanding would be the driver of decisions and ethics* and could have a monumental impact on the behavior and emotions of those who find themselves leading business organizations.

In addition, it will become evident that cycles are the root cause of that which moves ideas from thoughts to communication to physical manifestation. For it is in our understanding through the expanding hierarchies of knowledge and information about the natural building block of cycles that we will more effectively impact that which is physically created.

Within the process of moving ideas into physical results, communication will also become a more important focus.

Communication is such a powerful tool that the saying "words are like cannons" will become even more appropriate in the business world. As we move away from serving notice within communication to one that helps facilitate knowledge and information, it will become more important that we choose our words carefully — especially the words we use to stimulate the creative process in the role we play as leaders.

What this means in the management of emotion, especially negative emotion, will be our ability to drop one accepted curse word in a playful and public manner and influence attitudes. This playful communication could have the impact of eliminating fear in the people receiving the communication. It may even motivate them to go forward with courage instead of with fear. Only one word and our impact on other's creative/creation process* can place the company within a whole new stream or direction of growing the value* the company creates. Just one word.

An additional leadership skill that will develop in the future will be an awareness of the cyclical nature of the uncontrollable stream of thoughts that flow through the mind as shown within the ten second test*. An understanding of the cyclical nature of an individual's stream of thoughts between positive and negative will help in understanding the needs of the individuals to whom the leader is communicating. It will help attune the leaders to the appropriate time to use that curse word as they automatically move to dispel issues of fear within the person receiving the communication.

This understanding or awareness of the positive and negative cycles within the stream of thoughts is influenced by those around us. It will place us in a position to see what is created within a company as the result of the total group's creative thought cycles. It should be understood that what is created within the company is the relationship between employees and customers and how they understand and influence each other.

It will be in this awareness of positive and negative thought cycles that leaders will begin to understand the importance of diversity in the creative thought process. This includes diversity in both their employees as well as the diversity within their customers' buying motives. They will know that the ability to manage creativity from a multiple perspective of excellence will become paramount. Leaders will also identify that lack of this skill set will lead to their obsolescence.

Hopefully, the use of fear in the above illustration will cause you to rethink or evolve your leadership philosophy.

New millennium thinking, or what I call 180-degree thinking, grew out of observing that fear has historically been a powerful motivator that leads to less than optimum results. It was my experience that companies experiencing poor competitive and profitability performance reflected a leadership process that increased the level of fear unnecessarily within its participants.

When my job required turning a company around competitively, a major objective of mine was always to move the leadership style to minimizing fear and the impact it had on employees and their creativity. This was accomplished by refocusing the leadership group. Within the planning process, I would have them focus on client relationship systems, product line enhancements, and other issues of competitiveness rather than utilizing a typical strength and weakness analysis and criticism from past decisions. All of the activities were focused on eliminating fear associated with poor performance and the impact it has on creativity.

Fear will be recognized more in the future as a destroyer of creative conciseness, despite its power as a motivator and stimulus for physical action. Fear also destroys the process within the business entity that leads to the highest levels of value creation.

The leadership goal in the future will be to develop an organization that is driven by self motivated employees who truly believe their jobs to be vocations rather than by self- and organizational-limiting individuals that are driven by fear. The question to ourselves at this point should be, "As leaders, who do we attract to ourselves — advocates or adversarial employees?"

As we develop and refine our leadership communication skills, we gain an understanding into the diversity of each person's knowledge base. A broadening definition of appropriate behavior will be required for a leader to remain objective in order to impact that employee's knowledge base most effectively. It will be this understanding that will prevent the waste of time and creative energy so prevalent today.

A discussion of competence versus incompetence as an absolute demonstrates a lack of awareness into the workings of the physical world. Understanding why organizations move through their natural cycles from an objective view point will be a skill required by leadership.

How will we as leaders develop this skill or vision? It will be developed through increased awareness. Some basic ideas, concepts and tools to accomplish this leadership objective will be in the following chapters.

To say it simply, this book is about managing awareness* in the new millennium. It is about personal growth that comes as a result of your increased awareness. I will keep it short, because your time is important.

Preface

*Definitions, page 153

**Bibliography, page 193

***Root ideas, page 144

When one of the leading business books of 2000 began with the statement "...the Buddhists are right: nothing is permanent and everything is interdependent...", it was time for us business participants to step back and ask what is going on with business theory and practice in this new and evolving millennium? When did we start quoting spiritual dogma as opposed to the likes of Taylor and Maslow **? In turn, how and why are Taylor and Maslow more relevant today than when they developed their theories of productivity and a personal hierarchy of needs more than 70 years ago?

It is also interesting that the above quote comes from the business practitioner David Pottruck, President and CEO of Charles Schwab and Terry Pearce, founder of Leadership Communication from their book *Clicks and Mortar***.

How does the above statement of change and interdependence apply to you? How and why are you going to benefit from the material you get? Moreover, what you see or understand today should change tomorrow and the day after that, and the day after that. If it doesn't, we fail to grow.

It is in our evolving understanding of this human condition that our behavior is directed until we learn that everything is interrelated.

When this spontaneous realization of large "A" awareness of interrelatedness occurs, it leads to our ability to be involved but detached. We can exert emotion with objectivity without our ego sense* involved in the result.

It also results in our becoming more aware of our true role and the impact we have on this constantly changing physical realm. It will be through this perspective that our creative/creation abilities will grow exponentially.

The point is made again; our perception of reality will be constantly evolving, moment by moment changing 180-degrees with one new piece of information. For example, for every circumstance we define as a problem, the prospect of solving or eliminating its impact is minimized if we do not understand the problem is the effect of other decisions on past problems. This means that as provincial problem solvers, we have historically solved the effects of other problems, and those problems are interrelated within whatever our current attentions are focused. This is especially true if we believe that our past decisions must be justified from a right/wrong perspective.

Although there is nothing new about the fact that our problem solving process should deal with a problem's historical cause and effect chain, what should be gained is an increase in large "A" awareness. It is important to understand that these multiple cause and effect problem chains* will impact current decision behavior as we commit to our decisions and lose objectivity. Increasing awareness will impact behavior in terms of what decisions are important and if the leader focuses on their own egocentric needs projected onto the company. This is as opposed to the needs and desire patterns of all individuals touched by the company.

A pervasive problem within today's financial leadership and a root cause* of a very myopic approach to ethics and standards can be equated to the short term (less than one year) focus on performance issues. This short term focus within financial and accounting theory and practice as a result of regulations and legal requirements become escalated by the demands of the investment community.

These and other issues relating to the financial leadership of a company have been part of the discussions of business/legal ethics and practices over the last 80 years leading to today's problems with leadership ethics. In particular, those discussions have been ongoing as to whether decisions that involve fees and prices were merited by the company and its leadership.

Finally, there has been the belief and discussion about the need to increase earnings and profitability due to a leadership thought process filled with multiple concerns and fears. Issues covering a spectrum of root causes for behavior are found within the personal service hierarchy (chapter 4, page 91) and the leadership hierarchy (chapter 5, page 100).

An example of the demands, problems, and thought process of a CEO or CFO might be to respond to the problem of not generating a large enough bottom line. They may decide to raise fees and prices on the company's service or products after being influenced by a number of perceived threats as well as the real problem of a flat or decreasing bottom line.

Example continued: We have decided to increase service charge fees because the investment community has indicated that we are not making as much money as our peers. In turn this will reflect on our stock price, which could result in our ultimate fear of losing the company through acquisition. This is why we have to increase fees without necessarily expanding value to the customer.

This decision would be justified by a financial review process that would include a study of the impact that a price increase would have on client buying patterns. This might be completed by an outside source to help justify the potential decision and would include estimates of lost or diminished client activity.

These estimates of usage drop-offs have been based historically on estimates of an assessment of clients and their negative behavior or change in buying patterns within a certain period of time after an increase was made. In so many cases, that period of time is short term in nature and could range from 30 days to one year at most. The result of that short-term period or focus would drive the decision to raise fees to the required level to obtain the needed (real or perceived) income.

To continue with this example, this activity is facilitated within the financial community by using past estimates of behavior change. The established model used to base the future result was also of short term duration and in many cases equated to a flat ten percent loss due to buying patterns.

The problem with this approach is the test period is too short to accurately forecast the actual loss.

Buying patterns are part of a longer cycle of behavior changes by customers, which results in the true and lingering impact not being discerned. This results in client usage loss many times above the industry standard of ten percent.

This begins a cause and effect chain of long-term behavior changes that impacts the company exponentially many times. Once a company begins to move down a road where decisions are based only on short term price and value, the company is managed into a blind alley. The blind alley effect impacts the companies attracting and detracting equation which leads to no real growth.

It is then easy for the company's leaders to become confused as to why the company is no longer competitive and increasing the number of customers served. This results in no real growth in profitability and leadership decisions that take on a vision and direction leading to no alternative other than to sell or dismantle the organization. Typically it is deliberate but in many cases forced under duress. In addition, the above situation leads to an intense environment with less than positive and proactive behavior and result.

Realizing these problem chains exist and must be managed within all strategic components of an organization will impact vision and awareness. Increased awareness of these chains is also required if a leader is to complete a turnaround within a negative environment as defined above.

These strategic components are what leadership in this new millennium should concern itself with when defining a new awareness within a company. It is presented to begin the process of building new dialogue and should impact (change) our definition of our primary activity as problem solvers. It should also heighten our understanding that our primary responsibility is the creation of value. It is not problems and the solving of those problems that should drive our actions on a daily basis.

Our actions should focus on the creation of value through BALANCED service to differing people components (i.e., customers, employees, suppliers, and shareholders). Within an organization, this strategy will take on increased importance when defining an exceptional leader.

How important is this 180-degree vision change in redefining our roles as leaders? Look at what happened 500 hundred years ago. The idea that resulted in our country's wealth and has become the largest fortune in recorded history was the idea the world was round. That one may arrive in the east by sailing 180 degrees in the opposite direction or west was the new theory and vision. That vision led to other visions and discoveries and so on until we find the Western Hemisphere occupying its place today as the center of world leadership and quality of life. All of these results were driven by issues related to business leadership and were a result of evolving individual desire patterns and creativity.

A more recent example is the railroad industry vision from a strategic standpoint. They focused on what they did

— which was to lay more railroad tracks — rather than on what their customers needed — the most effective transportation of their products. Awareness came too late to railroad executives that they were in the transportation business and not the railroad business. A simple mistake, easily made, and so devastating to the premier business practitioners 70 plus years ago.

When others look back over the next 1,000 years to the turn of this new millennium, there will be a number of major breakthroughs in business theory and practice that will have revolutionized the role leaders have within their respective companies.

I believe one of the breakthroughs will center on managing awareness. Included with increased awareness will be the reality and understanding that the root cause of unlimited potential to create something of value for clients will exist due to expanded individualized desire patterns.

These expanded desire patterns will be due to increased knowledge and information within the four Ss covered later within this book. As we are exposed through knowledge and information to this world and the diversity of its experiences, we will find our lives expanding in quality and length.

Summary

This book is about understanding with large "A" awareness that decisions, words, and thoughts are like creative/creation cannons. They are powerful and are the building blocks of the "attracting" and "physicalization" process.

Applying the Buddhists' statement of "interdependent" and in turn "interrelated" found at the beginning of this preface can be experienced as follows — the only way to know that we can direct creative energy to someone else and to receive that creative cannon back is to actually do it and experience the phenomenon. (Dr. Kam Yuen **)

In the future, leaders will have developed an enhanced awareness of desire patterns* as they expand their ability to identify with clients and markets. Their creative/creation activity will anticipate these evolving desire patterns. They will also be able to see how each unique industry is interrelated and impacts others. The result will be to research and develop only those products and services that provide the fulfillment of these evolving needs. The effect of this increased efficiency will accelerate the creation and satisfying of individual and market desire patterns. Value created will grow significantly.

Because of the value that will be available based on expanded desire patterns, consumers will consume many times squared the output that the business process provides today. Powerful demand consequences are evolving and are almost limitless to those leaders who are focused.

Most important, an individual's leadership, ethics* and perspective will change with the dawning of this prosperity consciousness. It will result in the ability to function from the appropriate levels and standards that transcend any and all discussions of ethics today. A leader will become self-driven from an ethics perspective and his/her behavior will become exemplary.

CHAPTER

1

Introduction

*Definitions, page 153

**Bibliography, page 193

***Root ideas, page 144

Author's note: Please read the Student Summary in chapter eight, starting on page 147. To facilitate your review of the book's concepts read Appendix B page 181, then consider the schematic on page 22 regarding hierarchies.

The author would have the student review concepts which begin to move the student towards understanding how powerful the business function can become at increasing the quality of life for everyone, especially over time.

Read quickly through the entire book. If you have mastered a speed reading technique, then use that process. This is highly recommended due to the nature of the material covered and the natural tendency of the mind to move in linear fashion from one idea to another in the assessment and judgment of each, without the reader having current access to all the information presented throughout the entire book. This linear approach would be a mistake. The ideas presented in the last few chapters will impact your perspective on ideas presented in the beginning of this book and are interrelated.

Then reread the book in depth as you are so moved. It is also important to become more exposed to authors such as these mentioned throughout the book and in the Bibliography section. The book can be considered a guided meditation on leadership, strategy, ethics, business and the value that is created within business activity.

This book is about awareness* (read Student Summary, page 147) and the role it plays in significantly increasing our quality of life and our ability to create value for ourselves and others. In the Management Hierarchy on page 117, awareness is the highest level for us to manage. How do we manage awareness? The answer is through awareness. For example, a technique that is used to begin the process of expanding our level of awareness is observing what we think and detaching ourselves from that observed. Our ability to detach from our ego sense* will result in mastery over a more powerful creative/creation process* within ourselves and others.

To increase the quality of life for you and everyone you touch, begin by observing your mind's stream of thoughts. The goal is to understand the why and how of your reactions to what is happening around you. By expanding your awareness of a broader definition and nature of ethics you will become a more successful business participant. Reading through this book with an objective view of what is being presented will give the reader the greatest benefit.

Once you have finished reading the book, it is recommended that you pay attention to those positive and negative situations in which you find yourself becoming emotionally intense. Observe your thoughts and ask yourself these questions: Why do I feel the way I do about what is being said or what is happening around me? What learned standard is making me feel that way? Is my reaction driven from the positive or negative aspect of my emotion as a result of that standard? You may find that your actions and reactions, judgment and emotions, behaviors and actions are anchored in your ethics, standards and beliefs. What you will find over time is that however anchored we are in our ethics, standards and beliefs that cause our actions, reactions, judgments and behaviors, there is always room to creatively see things from a different more expanded perspective and awareness. This vision also expands our alternatives and places us in a position to choose how we react to that which is seen or observed. I call this 180-degree vision.

One of the objectives of this book is to help you evolve your leadership perspective by identifying the various elements responsible for individual behaviors. Another objective is to provide you with a Strategic Management Process that facilitates a balanced approach and a "back to the basics" assessment of a company's business model. This will apply whether the company is a startup or a Fortune

100 giant.

So where do you start? Begin by studying the four hierarchies presented throughout the book (exhibit 1.1, page 22). Then relate them to your "frame of reference" and assess how you could apply them to positively impact what you create in the future. Gradually your focus will move away from judging what is seen with a two dimensional right/wrong or good /bad vision of problems to one where your knowledge and information increases more powerful alternatives. It is understanding that the root cause of problem situations are just part of the natural physicalization* process by which hierarchies are formed, modified and grow.

HIERARCHIES:
INTEGRATED RELATIONSHIP

| MANAGEMENT HIERARCHY Page 117 | ⟷ | LEADERSHIP HIERARCHY Page 100 |

LEADERSHIP AWARNESS (vision)

| PERSONAL SERVICE HIERARCHY Page 91 | ⟷ | KNOWLEDGE HIERARCHY Page 124 |

Exhibit 1.1

Although this book is written for the business leader,

anyone can adopt a leadership vision in whatever role they have. It can be considered a reference or manual for anyone who is creating something of value — whether it is in the nurturing of a child or another human being, as well as in developing a product or building a community.

The original title of this book was *Leadership Focus Within the New Millennium: Surviving a Successful Career.* During my 35 years in the banking industry, too often I witnessed presidents and CEOs meet the objective of success as defined by others while not fulfilling their lives as human beings. The negative impact on their quality of life was experienced also by the many that surrounded CEOs and had sacrificed aspects of family. Especially traumatic was the loss and regret these leaders experienced when their careers ended and they finally had the time to reflect on their accomplishments.

A primary reason for this regret was the emotional intensity and significant time committed that was not available for other aspects of their lives. The driving force behind this expenditure of emotional energy and time was the fear associated with the possibility of failure. This message was delivered by being told that they were either personally liable for failure or directly responsible for how their companies performed.

This fear of poor performance induces emotional stress and will often become the root cause of poor health. This is especially true when the fear and stress occur over a lifetime on a sustained basis. As you focus on your priorities, it is important to be aware of the impact emotional stress has on the body and its potential role in an early demise. When you detach from fear, you place yourself in a position to understand that you have the ability to choose the emotional environment in which you place yourself.

As this book developed, the objectives of it evolved to include topics that would help explain the intensity of both positive and negative behavior within the work situation. It included such subtle ideas as our loss of personal freedom within our work environment through our expanding or contracting roles and authorities. Additionally, how we strive to maintain or expand our personal freedom leads to the belief that it is important to always prove and defend our decisions as correct, even to the detriment of others. It can force unnecessary reorganizations or the eventual sale of a company once leadership decisions move a company down a road or direction driven primarily from a competitive or financial focus. Another example is the tendency to implement poor product and service systems tied primarily to financial issues rather than evolving customer needs and desire patterns.

In understanding where business ethics begin, it is vital to understand how our belief system is ingrained in every thought and action... and is constantly changing moment by moment and with time and circumstances. It is important to understand that our belief system is piloted by our desire patterns within our own physical, mental, emotional, and psychological levels of understanding of which we are not aware in most cases. For example, how we behave ethically can be the result of our perception of issues as subtle as our feeling of entitlement due to our level of expertise and where that entitlement comes from within us, such as when we take personal responsibility for our clients as our personal standard. How our perception of issues, ethics and opportunity can then become confused as new levels of entitlement are developed from our experience and awareness.

At what point does our personal feeling of entitlement supersede the company's statement of entitlement within their policy, rules and regulations on how we create value and treat clients? Are customers always right and when should our decisions be driven by the perspective that the ends justifies the means? Does the ends justify the means apply when it comes to trying to change the natural cycles of value creation within a company's bottom line so that it appears linear in nature, something so prevalent today from a leadership standpoint as they respond to accounting and investment issues?

What the above questions are meant to stimulate is our understanding and awareness of how subtle our individualized standards are that always drive our behavior and ethics.

Another point of awareness is understanding that a business transaction, both its profitability and the environment that supports the transaction, are subject to the natural laws of cycles and hierarchies. These cycles are found within all physical and nonphysical processes and include phases that move back and forth between what is perceived as negative and positive situations and activity. These positive and negative cycles are pervasive and found within everything from the atom as a basic building block of nature to attitudes we have for each other. These cycles expand and contract desire patterns of individuals on the physical, mental, emotional, psychological levels that lead to buying patterns.

One of the main reasons why activity within the development of new products or services may seem fool-proof from an intellectual standpoint, but fail to satisfy a potential customers desire patterns is because of changing cycles. This results in wasted time, forced transactions and minimal value being created. When we tie into evolving clients' desire patterns, we find that results are transactions and business volumes that happen effortlessly, almost without logic. The personal computer and the resulting need to simplify its use through evolving software is an example of an industry giant that almost defies logic.

Another objective of this book is communicating the knowledge and information that can change the human condition by focusing on new standards and ethics. One powerful standard should be for each of us as business participants to refocus on life from a longer and broader perspective. This focusing should be accompanied by a frame of reference* that seeks to maintain objectivity in our business situation. Objectivity allows us to dissociate emotionally. This begins the process of minimizing the trauma of stress and its impact on the physical systems that over time deplete the body of its vitality and function.

Leadership: Where Business Ethics Begin emphasizes those issues that minimize the negative impact of stress. This minimizing will be accomplished by understanding the importance of establishing new standards. An example of this is the situation in today's business environment that is preoccupied with short term performance. This short term focus is driven in part by the demands of the investment community, resulting in standards of how much value is correct from a competitive and ownership perspective and not on how value is evolving and changing within a business transaction.

There are many reasons that short term performance drives behavior. One reason for the importance of short term performance was acquired in our formal educational experience. Our educational groundwork focused us into individual competitiveness with each other from class ranking to bell curves and sports. The top students had found that they were best at competing intellectually with each other rather than being focused into a powerful service perspective to obtain cum laude status. They then took that competitive perspective into the work environment as the basis for their ethical perspective.

How do we start to evolve the ethic that drives our understanding and behavior? What is the nature of the new focus that drives objectivity leading to changes in vision and behavior? The following can begin that process:

Focus on understanding the value needed to help expand our clients' life cycles and how their needs will grow exponentially. This focus can be completed within all industry sectors! Focus on either becoming a root cause of those expanded life cycles or in providing the required support for that extended life.

New Personal and Business Standard defined: It is my contention that within a person's career and life span there are three evolving life stages.

The first of these stages can be considered the initial learning stage and begins at birth. Knowledge is acquired relating to issues involving the physical world and society. In gaining knowledge of these activities we learn how to create value and a means of participating in a chosen livelihood. The duration of this period lasts for roughly 40 years.

The second stage is the period when that person takes what has been learned and applies information with precision to the direct activity of creating something of value within a business or career activity. This will lead to this person having the ability to provide for themselves and others by relying on their knowledge and expertise. This period will also last about 40 years.

The third stage of a person's life cycle is when they lead by teaching and instructing those that are experiencing the first and second stages of their life. They would also form a deeper understanding of their relationship and interrelatedness with all that is being expressed during their journey within this life and time. Although this sharing activity should be emphasized during the third period, it should be ongoing throughout a person's entire life. Remember, knowledge and information is gained within the journey and not in the result or destination. Ultimately, the person through extended involvement in business and industry sees the expansion and growth in knowledge hierarchies and cycles within each industry as a response to desire patterns of people over time.

It should be apparent that although these evolving periods might overlap for as many as ten years, the new standard will be that on average an individual will have a total life cycle of 120 years. As one looks at the length of life cycles being experienced, most people fall short of a healthy life cycle of 120 years. It is becoming more apparent due to our understanding of the physical body and its connection to the mind that emotional stress in general, and business related stress in particular, are root causes of our shortened lifespan. A broader and more complete discussion of stress can be found within the book *Healthy Aging* by Dr. Andrew Weil, M.D. **

It is also my contention that a shortened life is due to a lack of knowledge and information. An example of this with large "A" awareness is an understanding of the time it takes for an idea to become physical within the physicalization process. Our attempt to force that process into a shorter timeframe is a major cause of stress.

By evolving one's understanding of the root causes and natural laws that drive this physical world, the length of a person's life cycle will extend. The question then becomes what ideas and issues are faced by each of us from a physical, mental, emotional, psychological, and psychic level that result in a shortened life experience.

The answer is how and where we spend our time and energy. The majority of our time is preoccupied with creating value for ourselves. This points out the critical role that business and the leadership process can enhance during the next 1,000 years. It is evolving, and if we look back at the last 150 years it can be seen that business and leadership within business has expanded their focus on social responsibility.

It could also be argued that this evolving role has been due more to the leader's ego satisfaction and resulting regulation rather than to a powerful service perspective. The perceived role of increasing the quality of life and the resulting longevity of the people we serve might be considered a happy accident, and was not at the forefront of most individuals' objectives. This does not negate the fact that the average life expectancy has increased to the levels being experienced today.

So how does one manage "awareness" within the management hierarchy in chapter six? The following is a brief discussion of an important idea that will impact awareness of everyone who will take the time to understand and discern an increased understanding of the sources of knowing

* as a root cause of vision, our standards and our behavior as a result of that vision.

Two Types of Knowing: There is knowing... and then there is Knowing. Much of the difference between the two is the source of knowledge along with its completeness. How you determine what type of knowing you are experiencing is a result of expanding awareness. This expansion in awareness is being experienced by all of us due to the explosion in knowledge and information.

The ability to access information and knowledge from the correct source of Knowing at the appropriate time is critical. It can transform a person's vision. This constantly evolving vision leads to decisions that are 180 degrees apart from what one might normally make. It results in the ability to understand how much validity to place on past knowledge as acquired through conscious mind activity as defined below.

The first knowing is the gathering of information with the conscious mind activity. Our reliance on information and its completeness is heightened by the efficiency of this mental activity that is driven by the cognitive ability measured by our IQ. This would include how efficiently we acquire and store, rank and judge information. It is where we think we physically create, build, and change form and function. To an extent this is true, although the source and motivation for creativity is not what we may think it is. This is principally where business theory and practice has spent the last 60 years. Formal business theory and practice has been involved in the act of trying to understand through conscious mind activity, that which is happening around us and its physical result.

The above is driven by our capacity as well as society's capacity to know through conscious mind activity. There are two types of individuals who have been involved in this capacity to know: participants directly involved in the creation of value (business practitioners), and participants who are responsible for observing and teaching (consultants and educators) the next generation of business leaders.

It can be observed through conscious mind activity that business theory and behavior have focused on defining, controlling, and understanding what has happened physically within the business arena. This leaves many of the root causes of what we are experiencing being perceived as unmanageable with any degree of accuracy. An example of this idea is found within the old management aphorism, "If you cannot measure it, it cannot be managed."

This perspective on physical issues is primarily due to the fact that the above physical result is observable by the five senses, the root cause of conscious mind input.

The focus on managing physical activities and results described above is now in the process of changing as leadership and business theory are evolving with the many breakthroughs being experienced within the four arenas covered by the Four Ss. These Four Ss include science, strategy, spirituality, and service and will be defined further in chapter two.

One of the most important abilities a leader will have in the future will be to possess an ongoing focus on the conscious mind activity and the process by which streams of thoughts flow through his or her mind. This activity of observing conscious mind thoughts has been presented within many spiritual traditions. The books *The Power of Now* by Eckart Tolle**, and *Awakening Loving Kindness* by Pema Chodron** should be considered as sources of additional insight. Most important will be a leader's ability to discern the impact positive and negative emotions have as a way of directing an enhanced creative/creation process. This ability to discern and impact emotions will help minimize the natural tendency for the conscious mind activity to develop motives other than satisfying desire patterns for customers. Another objective of this book is to begin a dialogue between people that will lead to techniques to accomplish that evolution in vision.

As we go forward with the above ability to focus on conscious mind activity, the diversity and awareness of hierarchies and cycles will become more pronounced. Our ability to understand these will range from the most minute, such as the cell cycle within the body and how this cell function impacts life and health, to as large as the hierarchies that come with understanding the impact business education has in shaping our thought process, standards and ethics within our formal schooling and in life. These cycles and hierarchies from cell function to business knowledge and theory are a result of our capacity to know through large K knowing.

The second type of knowing or large K knowing is what is changing at a rapid pace. This capacity for knowing can be observed within focus and understanding of educators and consultants that observe within the business arena. An example of the evolution in leadership can be found within current business issues such as the expanded focus on diversity. This includes an understanding of the importance of diversity within our racial, religious, gender and ethical perspectives and how they impact insight into evolving desire patterns. In addition, the acceptance of diversity as a creative right within a person's individualized approach to value creation is becoming a larger catalyst for organizational change than ever before. How we accept and respond to diversity in thought, word and deed from a leadership perspective is impacted and communicated through our decision on issues that lead to correct action. These decisions are driven by whether we are functioning from small "k" or large "K" knowledge and understanding about diversity.

The second Knowing is spontaneously accessed by the act of just knowing. It historically has been called intuition, gut, vision, or the voice within. This second Knowing comes from a source other than the five senses and intelligence. Its source is super conscious mind * discussed further in this book. The term super conscious mind is an idea that is a result and expansion of large "K" knowing within the Four Ss explained within chapter two. It is also a more important source of ethics and behavior that can result in a truly objective perspective. True objectivity will be a major factor that enhances value creation and the creative thought process that will evolve during this next 1,000 years.

Large "K" knowing has to do with the ability to cultivate the idea of knowing and has been associated with the idea of clear understanding and experience.

The difference in focus between the two types of knowing can be partly explained in terms of understanding the importance of what the mind knows. An example of this is that less importance is placed on the rightness of what is currently known and more importance is placed on being open to the creative thought process and the resulting solutions that come out of the process. The result of this understanding does change behavior significantly by minimizing our need to prove our rightness. This can be called a 180-degree change in both awareness and vision.

An example of a 180-degree change in awareness is an understanding that the small "k" knowledge activity is responsible for those ideas that flow through our minds while large "K" knowledge controls our body function and what is presented to us in life. The magnitude of knowledge and information we possess from the super conscious mind activity can be demonstrated by the impact it has on the physical body, where control and process includes everything from the billions of nerve impulses responsible for everything from involuntary heart action to controlling the five cell functions within each cell at one level and our ability to walk at another level or hierarchy. The super conscious mind is truly the root cause of our ability to function over-all in this physical world.

The understanding of how the body creates for itself and permits function within our world and our responsibilities as part of that function is part of the expanded definition of Spiritualism* within the Four Ss. The most important point of awareness for us as business participants is an under-standing of our capacity to function within this physical body with all of its attributes and abilities as part of the business creation process.

It is essential to recognize that we have the ability to determine function of these nonphysical ideas, phenomena or energies. We have both the control and freedom that leads to expanded awareness. It is especially important that we understand the fact that everything is changing at a me-teoric rate as a result of evolving desire patterns found in all of us.

This book is meant to help change the reader's perspec-tive or frame of reference* when dealing with current busi-ness life. Why is this important? It is important because with this change in awareness, what is seen will be altered and our assessment of what is happening around us will become keener. This keener focus or the increased aware-ness that results will release much of the confusion and false ideas concerning not only our environment but the change that is ongoing. The most important point is our ability to accept the idea of change without emotion and judgment. By putting on a pair of awareness glasses, the view of your life will also change.

Change* is activity that permits us to build the necessary hierarchies needed to deal with the cycles found within the physical world. It is that understanding and awareness of our physical world that provides the constructs for our ideas and energy that are constantly changing. It is the awareness that it is impossible for our physical environment not to change. Only if all particles stopped within their function or cycle would we have no change (Deepak Chopra**). It is part of the life we live within the human condition.

So how do we apply this natural law of change to our understanding of business? Business or the ability to create something of value for another has always been involved within the activity of determining what people desire that leads them to a transaction. This activity had been determined through trial and error by what people had physically purchased prior to that particular moment and defined industry structure. The amount and quality of information on a particular product or service determined what people would strive to obtain.

From the time we began to move from complete independence in what we consumed to an existence of complete dependence on others for even our basic physical needs, individuals began to evolve their knowledge and information to determine what they purchased. This activity is preceded by their awareness leading to desire patterns that lead to business transactions that satisfy these basic needs.

It is in the fulfillment of these rapidly expanding desire patterns that business activity will evolve to a point that business participants will find the value they create for themselves will grow exponentially over their life, as well as over the next 1,000 years for people in general.

Chapter Summary:

There are a number of trends that are happening today that will result in a limitless need for the value that is created by business. The idea of finite or limited potential for companies and the people who participate in this value creation activity is incorrect.

As business leaders learn to tap into the evolving desire patterns and needs of us who consume value, they will find themselves in a position to anticipate those needs. The result of that awareness will create focus for the business process to grow in the future to meet and fulfill these needs. This chapter covers some of the more than twenty-plus root ideas*** presented throughout the book. I hope that the readers' awareness and frame of reference will be impacted by reviewing these root ideas and that their vision leads to an understanding of how future prosperity can occur and expand their quality of life and everyone they touch.

Finally, once you have read through the entire book, visit Appendix C for additional discussion on issues within chapters one and two. Appendix B also includes a quick reference guide for the book.

2

New Millennium Leadership Focus: Integration of the Four Ss

*Definitions, page 153

**Bibliography, page 193

***Root ideas, page 144

Focusing on what is happening around you and then detaching from the result was one of the main ideas presented in chapter one.

An additional idea was to focus on how our business models were evolving to help clients increase the quality of life and its average length to 120 years. The objective would be to enhance those models into a longer perspective that lead to an increase in the quality and length of life of individuals touched by the company.

The vision and new standard in chapter one was one that every industry and company could begin to focus on to evolve their business model in general, as well as influence every transaction specifically. What makes the focusing on expanded lifetimes powerful is that the requirements needed to expand life cycles will result in increased desire patterns. That increase in desire patterns will fuel an almost limitless demand for business services and value creation.

This longer term vision can then be simplified by integrating a company or industry strategy with our own personal strategy. An actual example of this can be taken from the financial services industry where mortgage transactions are difficult, confusing and have serious impact on the clients they serve. A simple but powerful personal statement of strategy of a person within the mortgage company's sales and relationship group would be to make these difficult transactions "painless" to the customer. To support that relationship mortgage person, a company might evolve and focus their operational business model to fulfill all the control requirements facing the institution with a transparent process to the client. This would also help begin the process that would move the organization away from a current leadership focus on poorly timed and executed transactions. It would be replaced with a focus on the impact of a transaction on the client over time. Based on the current situation in that industry dominated by fear based models, that company's business model would focus on knowledge and information as a model and would move that organization many years ahead of the industry.

The Four Ss of the new millennium include a focus on and integration of strategy*, science*, spirituality*, and service*. This focus includes an evolution of what these four words mean. Understanding the depth of these ideas or components should suggest to those reading that expanding definitions will be a necessary part of expanding awareness. This understanding will be needed by those responsible for managing business entities and activity in this new millennium.

This evolving awareness should also influence our understanding of what we believe we are in control of within the business environment and what we are not. It should influence our understanding of what is responsible for success and our role within the multiple cause and effect chains we manage. This will lead to how we define success in the future.

We can start the awareness process by building definitions that expand our understanding of the Four Ss. The future focus in leadership will be in developing strategy that is integrated with the evolving knowledge and information hierarchies found with issues relating to science, spirituality and service.

Definition: Strategy*: Strategy is organizing and digesting varied aspects of a company vision and how and what it creates as value. Through this vision comes the awareness that much of the implementation of strategy is the process by which we manage the gaps between what is current and what is to be developed. These gaps include everything from unrealized desire patterns in all of us to the physical creation of the products and services to be offered and delivered.

A more detailed definition of strategy is the activity by which we focus on those components that are both macro (group) and micro (individual) in nature. These activities and ideas define the actions that make up a company's understanding of how it creates value for clients, employees, suppliers, and shareholders. This includes maintaining balance among issues such as the company's marketing (product, pricing, communication and distribution processes), financial philosophy (the identification of the business from a monetary standpoint), to leadership and management processes that impact the operations and people who are touched by the firm's existence. As difficult as these issues are to define, it is important to know that when defined correctly, balance is gained that generates the greatest impact on physicalization or materialization of vision. What is being experienced today due to the lack of a balancing of the above issues is a focus on those activities that result in less positive impact on physicalization and value, or which have no impact on value creation.

So where does one begin? A good place to start is to look at how a company and its leaders construct and communicate their mission statement. This initial look can be most revealing about their awareness.

A mission statement that is preoccupied with a company's definition of itself or how it wants to be perceived shows a narrow understanding of where the main focus should be. An example of this can be found when terms such as premier or optimum service are used to define a future state of the company. These terms are constantly changing and will confuse rather than clarify the mission statement. The direction set is one that reflects the desire of the participants that are about the task of setting new standards for themselves. The type of standard is one that sets them apart from other industry participants. This is part of the natural competitive environment that businesses find themselves; it can ignore the reason for a company's existence.

It is important to understand at this point that the cycles of a company are a result of the cycles within an individual who leads or individuals who lead the company. The cycles within an industry are also a result of the individuals running the companies within an industry. From the poorly crafted mission statement focused on the company rather than the value it creates begins the cause and effect chain that results in defining the activities and people delivering that service, rather than the value they provide.

A good example is the medical industry, and how we refer to the top individuals in that industry. We call them doctors, which is in deference to the level of their education. In other healing cultures such as in eastern cultures the same experts are given the title of "healers" which refers to the service they offer other people. Although this difference between doctors and healers may seem subtle, the reality impacted by the practitioners of the healing arts expands the definition of their activities. That definition moves from a focus on the treatment type based on the symptoms that are physically apparent in the patient, to also changing the condition that is responsible for that poor health. They attempt to assist in the natural healing process so as not to set the condition in place for poor health to develop again in the future. What is added, in many cases, is the requirement to correct those weaknesses in the patients' systems.

The above scenario is not intended to isolate or offer up a judgment of good or bad within the best practices of a particular industry. It is my experience that medical professionals today are more focused on the result of their assistance in helping patients heal and are more predisposed to the giving of selfless service to help their patients than they have been in the past. It is also my belief that with so many industries today, there is truly a new age dawning of awareness and knowledge which is driving breakthroughs at an accelerated pace.

Definition: Science* A focused and simplified definition of science includes a stronger understanding and awareness of the physicalization process. The basic building blocks of light and atoms are impacted by the creative/creation process that we are responsible for as individuals and society/mankind.

There is an intricate but understandable set of laws and processes that are responsible for the physical world and that which manifests within it. Included in these laws of creation are laws relating to the mental, emotional, psychological, psychic, and spiritual realms. These are the realms in which we function. They are responsible for what manifests and which we are part of from a creative/creation process. Gene research is an example of a knowledge hierarchy that is expanding our understanding of how the conditions for a living organism develop and function.

One of these laws is the law of attraction*. It states that everything we experience is a result of what we are able to attract and accept. The law of attraction is directed by our desire patterns and functions within the process of creating the right circumstances based on what is being attracted. Like the involuntary functions in the body, we are normally not aware of this process. It is described in the works of Jerry and Esther Hicks** and their approach to instructing people with techniques that facilitate that attraction process. I have seen it used in the process of attracting individual buyers and sellers together that lead to transactions and the attraction of those transactions to individuals who use the process. This is a function of base desire patterns within each of us that influences an individual's inherent skills. Each of us is able to use these techniques to a greater or lesser degree.

Science also includes those theories and work being developed within the arena of quantum physics, such as those presented by Deepak Chopra.** He addresses the impact an individual's thought process has by anticipating what will happen when an atom is split. He states that what manifests from the void or space between the light particles that make up the atom changes with what is anticipated. In other words, how that which is anticipated within the new mass seems to manifest with no logic except that it was perceived by the scientists completing the experiment.

All expanding science and knowledge hierarchies will impact directly on business. It will result in the need to develop a more focused research and development process with an expanded role. Those heightened development roles will be the new standard that companies will have to maintain in order to remain successful. This is especially true if they address the topics of increasing the quality and length of life with all participants on all levels. An example of this applied is the medical industry's breakthroughs in cell and gene function and the parts they will play in impacting business activity.

The media and entertainment industry members are in a position to view themselves as having a responsibility to increase the velocity of human experience. The industry can facilitate the learning and experience process of its audience as part of the explosion in awareness. This awareness is part of the resulting leap in the volume of desire patterns in all of us. The M/E industry can also be responsible for the focus of this new millennium business theory and practice by impacting demand curves. All things are truly interrelated.

The awareness that results is a vision by the leader that science has become the focus within every field of endeavor from technology to engineering to behavior sciences. When focused on the impact their company can have with life and the human condition, the vision that results will move the function and application of the leadership process 180 degrees.

Definition: Spirituality* A more expanded definition of spirituality is the awareness and understanding of that which precedes and follows "physicalization." It is the focus on that which is responsible for the ideas that result in the materialization of ideas and thought. This knowledge and information of non-physical aspects of the physicalization process will result in enhanced value creation and has the potential to result in the development of that person who has awareness and insight as a skill set. He or she might be called a spiritual director within the new organization of tomorrow.

As stated in the definition of science, there is an intricate yet understandable set of laws and processes that are responsible for the physical world that manifests.

All major religious doctrines refer to different aspects of the creation process within the human condition. These range from individual health and care to helping individuals understand and give direction to appropriate behavior within society and towards each other.

This book has been developed to eliminate conscious mind judgment and the provincial religious belief that has had negative impact on the human condition. The physicalization of the negative realities that mankind has experienced has been due primarily to a mistaken understanding of the truth of spiritual law. What has manifested or has become physical is due to the conscious mind process and its two-dimensional vision.

Definition: Service* The root cause of any standard or ethic should be understood to begin with a more powerful understanding of service. A more powerful service perspective is the root cause of what it will take to evolve the issues of leadership suggested by the title of book *Leadership: Where Business Ethics Begin*. That being said, it is important to define what service is and in turn to provide a more focused definition of service within leadership. Service within human behavior is an important part of the human condition in which we find ourselves participating.

Service can be considered to be the creative thought process that is tied to other individuals' evolving desire patterns on the physical, mental, emotional, psychological, psychic, and spiritual levels of understanding and existence. These desire patterns result in the basic needs each of us has in this life cycle. These base needs can be very subtle and include the process to eliminate the ego sense* of separateness of everything in this physical world. Service also moves us to further understand why the Buddhists' statement that everything is interrelated is a statement of universal truth.

Once large A awareness is developed and maintained, the evolving skill becomes one of functioning within our expanded understanding. Our decisions reflect a much clearer awareness of evolving motivations of other individuals. This skill is driven from our new perspective and will eventually replace ego based motivations. By replacing our perspective with a sincere desire to serve others we reflect an understanding of our responsibility and interrelatedness to each other that can be found in most world belief systems.

It is also important to note that this is not a discussion of religions, but rather a discussion of the root cause of ethics and where these ethics originate in thought. It also communicates that as a focus in business strategy, it will be important to understand that integrating the Four Ss suggests that these seemingly disparate parts of our society's activities are really very much interrelated. They help us form an understanding for that which is happening around us and of our own evolving desire patterns.

A definition of service should be prefaced by the fact that like all ideas and processes within this physical world, the root cause of service as a standard is always changing and is as individualized as it is mass in nature. In other words, the individualized service related responsibilities of a business leader are significantly different than they were 100 years ago, or even ten days ago. Most important is the understanding that if one is not objective, it is very simple to be part of the behavior process that leads a particular leader to decide that deception within service motivations can be a natural ally, only to discover that it is a resulting foe. An ego based service perspective is also the reason most leaders do not survive even successful careers without suffering the silent agony of that which is lost within the normal career cycle.

The answer to the service reality in consciousness is to begin to build on the ability to be involved but detached. It is also important to eliminate that which has been defined as the ego sense and the vision that manifests from that perspective. In other words, to find oneself in the position of feeling extreme happiness and contentment from what has been of benefit to those we have served over our career cycle. It is important to move away from and not maintain or manifest our own desire patterns that seek to sustain the positive aspects of our ego gratification. Ego gratification comes naturally from acceptance of the counsel we give, the attention to our authority, the respect it commands, and of course the money.

Attachment to positive manifestations of authority, power, and its responsibilities is what led to the attachment to leadership by leaders. Unless one understands that the most subtle form of deception is self-deception, then what is experienced by the leader can take the form that seems like objective detachment. However, the leader is only functioning at a refined level of deception characterized by the conscious mind that sets up a narrow definition of leadership service and behavior that is also a subtle form of self deception. These realizations are normally only experienced after negative feelings of loss or impending loss are experienced and the accompanying grief is experienced over an extended period of time.

The only offsetting solution to this cyclical part of leadership and the leadership environment is to experience a breakthrough in awareness through focused contemplation of many aspects of this physicalization process — to transcend the desire to be of service for any gain on the physical, mental, emotional, psychological, psychic and spiritual levels that function together but apart. That person begins to see from a perspective that has been defined within the religious traditions as universal and unconditional love.

Chapter Summary:

The ability to gain insight and expanded awareness within the Four Ss that lead to understanding the discernment of these issues will be a part of the knowledge and information required by leaders in this new millennium. It will in turn lead to the ability to actively manage the creative/creation process in others and ourselves. This active management of the creative/creation process will lead to exponential growth in the productivity and value that a single person can manifest.

The growth in knowledge and understanding of the Four Ss will set the stage within this new millennium in business for a reality that enhances the quality of life for all who participate.

A more personal and simplified understanding of strategy tied to the major breakthroughs in all areas of science, along with a greater understanding and awareness of issues surrounding service and spirituality (how things become physical) will result in an explosion of growth in demand for both products and services by individuals. This will be a direct result of expanding desire patterns — a powerful future in which to be a creative participant.

Appendix C: Discussion points from chapter two. And expanded chapter summary.

3

180-Degree Vision

*Definitions, page 153

**Bibliography, page 193

***Root ideas, page 144

Out of expanding awareness comes what I have dubbed 180-degree vision*. This perspective includes seeing and understanding why both positive and negative aspects of the human condition exist and does not offer up judgment of that condition. All decisions within a business entity are affected by a leader's vision or understanding of what he or she believes to be happening around himself or herself, and how he or she will go about creating the structure and environment that leads to a transaction or sale.

In the future how well leaders accomplish that activity and understand the creation/creative process (as well as where to focus their attention) will be impacted by the ability to behave and make decisions within 180-degree vision.

At odds with the ability to function from a 180-degree perspective are the negative tendencies of the heart. For example, fear as delineated within the Buddhist tradition as one of the eight basic negative tendencies, and the behavior and decisions that manifest as a result of that negative ability or tendency of the heart is a primary deterrent of what I describe as 180-degree vision and leadership. Many accepted standards in business that address correct leadership behavior and focus are built on using fear as a root cause when motivating action within human behavior. It is one of the root causes of the current human condition found in business. In addition, the ability to correct a leader or individual that manages or reacts from fear will be an evolving skill set of future leaders in this new millennium. This is especially true as more awareness is gained through knowledge and information.

So what is 180-degree vision? It is the ability of the leader to see and understand what is happening around him or her and knowing that both positive and negative tendencies of the heart are cyclically affecting that which is seen. If a decision of the conscious mind is dominated by the negative portion of the positive/negative thought cycle, that decision will adversely impact events.

The most important way to manage that reality is for the leader to step back and observe with detached objectivity. It is with growing awareness and understanding that the hierarchies and root causes found within this book will permit detached objectivity to grow within individuals. This vision and objectivity results in the ability to maintain balance within an organization's strategic components that include issues relating to marketing, finance and leadership (tied to the service [page 91], leadership [page 100], and management [page 117] hierarchies found in chapters 4, 5, and 6). [see exhibit, page 22]

So how does a business practitioner begin to refocus a company on a more balanced approach to the management of value and creativity? The answer is by applying the schematic The Strategic Management Process and Risks on pages 56 and 57 to his/her company and industry situation. This visual outline of the components and issues within the definition and development of strategy helps begin to align conscious mind activity. What is even more important is that super conscious mind* activity can be directed within the creative process that is responsible for enhancing attracting issues within the physicalization process and focuses participants on a more targeted development process. A targeted development process facilitates the physicalization of a company's creative definition of how they create and expand value within their industry and process. Applying the above schematic to our situation should also help the reader understand that so much of what we do not see is just a function of enhancing awareness, vision, and knowledge.

STRATEGIC MANAGEMEN

Marketing Principles / Process

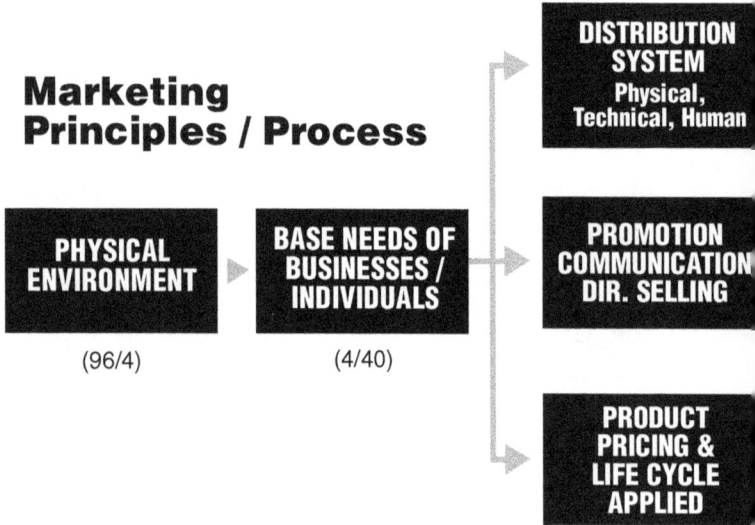

PHYSICAL ENVIRONMENT	**BASE NEEDS OF BUSINESSES / INDIVIDUALS**	**DISTRIBUTION SYSTEM** Physical, Technical, Human
(96/4)	(4/40)	**PROMOTION COMMUNICATION DIR. SELLING**
		PRODUCT PRICING & LIFE CYCLE APPLIED

CAUSE...EFFECT...CAUSE...EFFECT...CAUSE..

Financial Principles / Process

BANK BALANCE MAGNITUDES	**NUMBER OF BUSINESS UNITS / HOUSEHOLD RELATIONSHIPS**	**STRATEGIC RISKS**	**FINANCIA AND CRED RISKS**

CAUSE...EFFECT...CAUSE...EFFECT...CAUSE..

Management Principles / Process

MANAGEMENT HIERARCHY	**MANAGING RELATIONSHIPS**	**PRODUCTIVITY** (Individual Capacity)	**INDIVIC FOCU**

PROCESS AND RISKS

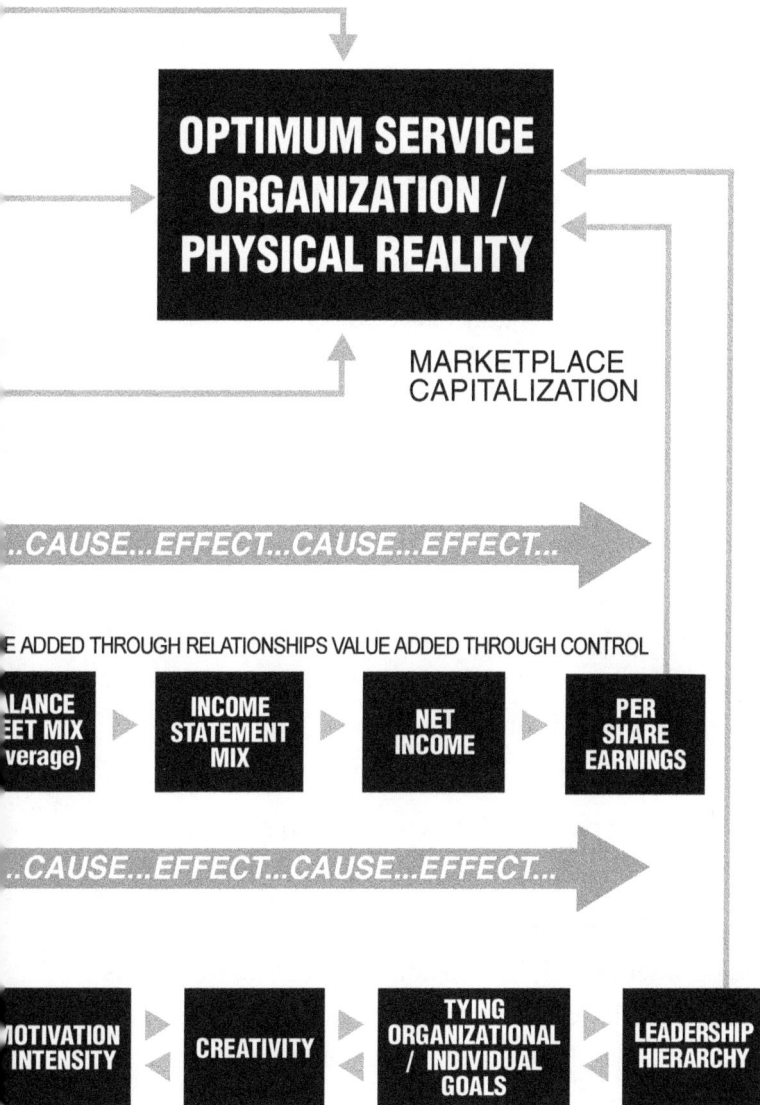

OPTIMUM SERVICE ORGANIZATION / PHYSICAL REALITY

MARKETPLACE CAPITALIZATION

...CAUSE...EFFECT...CAUSE...EFFECT...

E ADDED THROUGH RELATIONSHIPS VALUE ADDED THROUGH CONTROL

ALANCE EET MIX verage)	INCOME STATEMENT MIX	NET INCOME	PER SHARE EARNINGS

...CAUSE...EFFECT...CAUSE...EFFECT...

MOTIVATION INTENSITY	CREATIVITY	TYING ORGANIZATIONAL / INDIVIDUAL GOALS	LEADERSHIP HIERARCHY

57

The schematic is meant to summarize and simplify different components within the physical environment that defines why a company or industry exists and includes comprehensive marketing, financial/accounting, and management components as stated in the definition of strategy. It is from these standards that a company's ethic can be defined, evolve and grow.

There are also cause and effect lines that seek to represent the inherent nature of the physicalization process moving from the root causes on the left to the effects on the right, and which represent the cause and effect chains mentioned within the book. Within each of the disparate parts (represented by individual boxes) are the issues relating to cycles and hierarchy (quantified statistics below individual boxes in some cases) that are constantly changing and evolving as a result of desire patterns of all participants, and the creative/creation process within macro components of society (where society focuses within the human condition such as its evolving technologies and events) as well as individual patterns within each of us.

Also involved is the nature of our individual impact on each other as we participate in creating physical products and services for each other and in turn act as consumers.

If this sounds much like an example of the statement "everything is interrelated," it is meant to. The roles we play as leaders and participants are driven by the desire to participate and facilitate the physicalization process for everyone, both directly and indirectly, moment by moment, and over time. It is driven also by being involved in the development and satisfaction of desire patterns of all participants within society and the human experience.

It is the realization above that came to me as an undergraduate student while I walked through the grounds of my alma mater some thirty-plus years ago. I wondered if other students were so focused on being of service to others and on "saving mankind" that they should educate themselves as to how to create something of value for other people, something of value that would increase the quality of life and the human condition, a quality of life today for so many of us that was once reserved for kings and queens.

To explain the diagram further, included within the schematic under two of the boxes within the marketing section at the top are numbers that reflect the nature of the point of difficulty and the resulting base needs that each of us face within our individual financial situations, whether we are aware of them or not. It is within these physical realities as quantified with ninety-six/four (96/4) and seven/six (7/6) needs along with a directional statement of four to forty (4/40) that the framework of an organization focused on evolving how that major multifaceted industry could redefine how its business model focuses completely on the individuals and other companies as customers and clients that they serve. Within a large U understanding of what the above numbers represent is a 180-degree vision that would result in a business evolution as well as revolution (in terms of the financial services industry) in and of itself.

Additional issues that emerge from the marketing section include those comprehensive marketing components coined the Four Ps (product, price, place, promotion) some 50 years ago, that further define the company's approach to items that are part of the value creating and communication process.

As a point of awareness, it will be helpful to apply each respective area to your situation, company or industry to determine if that which is considered to be a statement of mission, policy or ethics, or other statements (i.e., annual reports, human resource statements, client brochures, relationship manuals for employees, decision criteria relating to client interfacing and definitions of roles and responsibilities) are pointed in the same direction. Is the written material focused on that person who is or persons who are recipients of the company's activity, or is it the company and its participants that are highlighted? Ask yourself, is there a standard for clients or the company? Then stop, slow the breathing by remaining still, and wait. Be aware of the cycle of your thoughts and feelings that follow. Wait, and listen to your thoughts. Then wait. Ask again, is attention focused on the company and company people (for egocentric reasons) in the company mission statement? Or is it client desire pattern focused? Then wait. Continue to observe what is going on around you. Then wait. Continue to observe your thoughts. Then wait. Observe your breathing. Then wait. Insight and awareness will dawn with patience and time as well as answers that impact with the power of realization into the conscious mind awareness.

Nowhere is there a more important catalyst of organizational cause and effect chains than a company's mission statement, so it is good to make sure that a leader starts that process or chain within a 180-degree management perspective.

The financial section in the center of the schematic includes components that move from left to right in a cause and effect type process that within the components drive both soft and hard dollar realities that in turn drive each respective component. The quantification of client and household/business financial data and the understanding of the multiple dynamics that form the cause and effect chain lead to shareholder value and market value of the stock. This should include the client's potential lifelong value to the company and its impact on the company's financial statements over time, including income as an absolute and as a cash flow, both within an individual transaction (tactical) as well as the total of all transactions over a client's life cycle (strategic). When these single and combined financial cash flows from the client to the company are integrated with the marketing mix activity what becomes apparent and offered within all four Ps results in transactions that seem to come effortlessly from nowhere.

It is in this financial management process that many of us were trained in the business schools dating from the 1960s and forward. It comprised a teaching of financial and accounting theory that shaped the ways we addressed a company's financial situation, more focused on accounting hard dollars (with those equations that taught us everything from net present value to yield to maturity).

What is most interesting to me from a beginning discussion about ethical behavior is what we were taught 35 years ago to help keep the company alive as it started to experience the financial cash flow difficulty or financial insolvency that leads to 80 percent of business bankruptcy. It amounted to activity that seemed unethical ("do not pay your bills"), which is accepted practice even today within the role that was developed for the CFO. This financial education helped groom students and the ethical system they were required to incorporate into their decision processes — an ethical system that started the cause and effect chain that has led to a breakdown of long-term relationships and loyalties, from client treatment to supplier purchasing activity and employee relations.

But even more important was how we were taught to look at a business situation and the process of solving problems — much like law schools that teach students to think about the process of law and the resulting standards or ethics that are created within that industry. As students of finance and accounting at both the undergraduate and graduate levels, our focus was placed on identifying a revenue stream and impacting it by either increasing revenues through price increases (or decreases to increase volume through share market moves from competition), or decreasing expenses involved with a product or services production or delivery.

An example of that financial thought process and considered an acceptable standard today is the practice of outsourcing activities for all expense items that a company might require based on the normal financial management/ budgeting process. The impact on value and service is known but is difficult to quantify.

Although there was always a discussion about product and service enhancement, it was usually regulated to responsibilities that would manifest themselves from the marketing activity and followed how the marketing areas must quantify their approach in the evolution of that activity to minimize the failure and cost of lost client relationships to research and development.

In addition, we were told also to focus on those activities that impacted positively on the process and the cost of each required process (i.e., McDonald's and the loss of their Special Sauce recipe during the 1990s as they tried to cut costs of the Big Mac). It was in the quantification of the physical components we were given that we subjected the environment to our models, just as the legal environment applied physical events and situations to precedence and past court decisions. It also led to slogans and statements by industry consultants that tried to simplify issues of value for these evolving financially trained leaders with statements such as "cheaper, faster, better" or in simplifying issues of value, which in turn led to commodity pricing within the research and development process, as well as product life cycle pricing overall.

An interesting cycle evolved over the next 30 years with those of us trained in what was considered the strongest of all business degrees — the finance degree. The need to grow within our careers from the basic financial requirements of a company to decisions that impacted leadership issues and ethics, along with the need and intimate understanding of the marketing components, resulted in most companies eventually becoming managed by those students of finance that became known as CFOs and company treasurers and as of today, CEOs. We focused our new leadership positions on issues of finance as the leading cause of value added and its definition. A situation that was two-dimensional in nature and in turn, the management systems that followed, as shown in the next section of hierarchy located at the lower section of the schematic, those ideas or issues covering management and leadership factors.

The brief delineation above is given as a point of awareness as to how the business sector evolves as a function of awareness of those who are educated and focused on learned theory, issues and resulting practice over time, and in turn learn to develop a narrow definition of appropriate business activities and leadership activities in managing the tactical as well as the strategic issues within their enterprises. These activities or processes can and do close out the creative/creation consciousness within the organization participants and result in the cycles of companies driven by an understanding of valued-added limited by predominantly short term hard dollar results and values.

The final major section of the strategic management process, as stated above, outlines major components that address leadership and management factors as part of the leadership process. Many of these components are addressed within the chapters that follow, but are also covered as a broad overview within this book.

Even when focusing on issues of ethics — which seem to be filled of late with a lack of positive results relating to corporations — their practices and their leadership will be impacted by a focus on 180-degree vision and in turn the nature of increased quality of their decisions. This would include decisions and activity concerning macro-level components starting at the governing level of a company's board of directors and shareholders to individual transactions with clients at the micro-level. This would also include micro-issues of attitudes and behavior of company employees towards clients. All are due to the level of vision related to the understanding of how value is created and how the physicalization process happens. This is all part of evolving 180-degree vision.

An example of this vision can be explained by an individual leader understanding with large A awareness that all behavior is subject to cycles and hierarchies within the individual. In particular, the simple reality that each individual is subject to positive and negative behavior and decision making cycles puts the leader in a position of understanding that necessary checks and balances can offset risks that distract from the creation of value.

This includes checks and balances that also involve the leader's own authority such as what is evolving today within corporate governance regulations, laws and ethical perspective. Every leader is subjected to his or her own cycles of behavior that can be defined as positive or negative when the most basic of litmus tests is applied – that which enhances value for others as opposed to being self-serving, no matter how justified.

Steven R. Covey ** with his vision and insight explains a person's "Frame of Reference" about what is happening around him or her and how that understanding can be changed by a single piece of information. This is an example of how a person's understanding can affect behavior spontaneously. Realizing that this change is happening on an ongoing basis transitions the physical outcome moment by moment as part of 180-degree vision and leadership behavior. It is a good place to begin to gain an understanding of how we are part of that which unfolds physically and how the Buddhists' statement that "everything is interrelated" does reflect the reality within this physical environment that the business function is responsible for functioning within.

The idea of 180-degree vision that leads to a 180-degree management focus and philosophy that will generate an organization focused on all components within its strategic situation's root cause can be illustrated by the following directional analogy.

As stated previously, 500 years ago the idea that resulted in the manifestation of wealth that has become the largest fortune in our recorded history was the concept that the world is round. The notion that one may arrive in the east by sailing 180 degrees in the opposite direction was a new focus or vision. That vision led to the discovery of the Western Hemisphere, which led to the development of new countries, which led to etc., etc.

180-degree management has much to do about the knowledge and information we receive and act upon. It is a function of what we do or do not see. As leaders, we are constantly asked to deal with the physical environment based on our understanding of how it manifests value. Our responsibility is to be visionaries and to help guarantee a future result. Keeping in mind the discovery of the Western Hemisphere and in turn the wealthiest country in the world — what will be the next concept that if addressed from the proper perspective will lead to the development of value within this physical world and that will have the same impact as that 180-degree reversal had 500 years ago that proved one could sail west to go east? A correct answer is not important but a moment to contemplate the idea is what can evolve or build on awareness now.

The next question might be as follows: Why is the following statement correct? "It turns out that the Buddhists are right: nothing is permanent and everything is interdependent," stated in the book *Clicks and Mortar* **. More important, is it absolutely correct overall, or correct in just those parts that we can identify with, understand or believe? Why did they make that statement? What were they trying to accomplish? Were they even aware that by using that statement in a validating way that they were validating the Buddhist spirituality in other statements of truth? Is it a statement of truth? Is truth on all levels the new focus within the new millennium leadership philosophy and ethical standard? What does that spiritual dogma have to do with corporate culture or anything relating to business theory and success?

The answers to the above questions are somewhere within their frame of reference or reality as well as within our own. In addition, whatever Pottrick's and Pearce's reality may be concerning the above questions, an important realization is that their reality is subject to change. This change will be a result of the evolving awareness due to new knowledge, information and ideas. It will be a result of feedback based on how we respond to their creative thought process and individual creativity as represented by the physical book and our response to it.

Our conscious reality and awareness can come to a higher level of understanding of interdependence as we understand and incorporate the result of their initiative and creativity. It will become interrelated with our behavior and decisions as their clients and the primary reason for the existence of their book — to impact our thoughts and behavior.

I finally realized within my own need to act on precedence (my formal finance education and experience) that Pottrick's and Schwab's statement on interdependence and interrelatedness are responsible for my decision to begin writing this book.

It can be very hard to discern that we are constantly impacting each other both directly and indirectly. It is impossible if one is not paying attention or doesn't understand that we are really observing a chain of events that is long and connects everything within the laws of this physical world. Just the process of how we accept and validate the idea that the Buddhists presented that "everything is interdependent" will result in a whole new spectrum of responses that influence our perspective.

Another point of awareness in the Schwab quote is the word "right," which is used as a powerful directional statement of absolute fact. A point of awareness here is in the chain of thoughts and logic under which we apply validation for ourselves. Within our framework of reference, especially if we are two-dimensional in our understanding or abstraction of how the physical world functions, we see things as right or wrong, proper or improper, ethical or unethical as absolute concepts.

Within this two-dimensional perspective it is even more important that we start with only ideas of absolute success — real or perceived — for that is what we have been taught from the beginning. All hierarchies should be built from prior hierarchies that have worked to a greater or lesser extent. In both business school and business career, it is in this validation process that many other perceived absolutes and realities begin to develop, including our ability to judge and establish standards from that judgment. That judgment is both consciously and unconsciously a necessary activity within so many fields of endeavor, including business. Whether we are aware of this validation thought process or not results in our ability to manage it and influence the process within others in our environment.

It is within this validation thought process or environment that we are led to our frame of reference to what is happening around us. What we believe is a function of where we have been and what we have been told. What we perceive to be right behavior and where our affinities and likes are focused is a function of where we have been and the standards that have been set for us. It is also that same environment in which we were raised that set the above standards for what we perceive as right and that make us happy while also being responsible for those standards that make us fearful and ashamed.

It is because of this intricate set of perceptions that we move to our judgments that lead to our decisions. If they are driven from a perspective that states that for every motive there is an ulterior motive, then our decisions will be even more filled with undesired and unintended consequences.

There is also a result at the opposite end of the Buddhists' statement of interdependence. This is where we feel we are truly separate and distinct from each other and other things, and will manifest and reflect the following: Our judgment is poor (180 degrees off) concerning environmental factors we deal with daily, as well as moment by moment.

The Buddhists' statement of change and interrelatedness should be the new awareness within our leadership focus and a major breakthrough in what we see. If it isn't, the result at best is a dual standard — one for oneself and one for everybody else. It is to say one thing and think something else, to condemn a like action that we condone within our own behavior — to adopt a conscious mind activity of absolutes that changes with the outcome.

To survive a successful career, we must become aware and transcend this thought process of two-dimensional thinking and acting. We can start by trying to stop setting false standards and living by them and projecting them on ourselves within our narrow definition of respectability. They do not reflect value, created or shared.

This intricate set of perceptions takes on an even more complicated reality or awareness if one expands the definition of the physical environment. This would include the physical, mental, emotional, psychological, psychic and spiritual environments, where all creative thoughts and creativity originates.

In addition, the fact is that our entire physical, mental, emotional, psychological, psychic and spiritual environments are subjected to hierarchies and cycles. One can see how the limitless parts of a problem and its solution are not two-dimensional, but limitless in dimensions. So what does this mean?

Every thought and every decision made takes on a multidimensional result from an immediate, short-term and long-term perspective, rather than a two-dimensional right/ wrong reality. That is one of the thousand reasons why the words "everything is interdependent" within the Buddhists' statement are true.

Note: It is in the daily implementation of the above truth statement by the Buddhists that the leaders of the future will expand their narrow definition of correct decision making, especially from external standards and judgment. When operating from this broadened vantage point, the practitioner will enhance the quality of their problem-solving result and focus.

New millennium leadership principle: The assessment of any decision from a provincial problem solving mindset is inadequate. An understanding that every decision from a hierarchy perspective is both right and wrong makes the problem solving mindset inadequate. This multidirectional impact can only be assessed as appropriate from within the individual who has obtained personal objectivity. It can only be assessed by that person who is involved, focused, but detached from the outcome of the decision, with all of their correct and incorrect motivations.

Although the above idea regarding self assessment might be considered a new business decision standard, its origin is rooted is the statement "to thine own heart be true."

It is in understanding that the heart lacks insight into truth most of the time that one begins to understand that the act of judging is without merit.

In addition, this self assessment is at odds with what we have been taught from an early age. We learned that in the final analysis we should look outside ourselves for validation of our thoughts and actions, as opposed to within ourselves. This is partly due to our acquired need to set and accomplish standards within every part of our lives as participants within evolving collective desire patterns — be it learning to tie our shoes to creating a new generation of business value.

Our simple need to be accepted or validated started the cause and effect chains leading to our ability to feel the effects of being judged and grew out of the training and development by those who first developed initial standards within our minds from our parents, family, teachers and friends.

This can be referred to as "consciousness playing off of consciousness," which is how the physical world manifests. This reality or awareness impacts both behavior and desire patterns and can be called a root cause in creating value within the new leadership philosophy. This awareness must be discerned and understood if we are to begin impacting awareness more effectively in others. These desire patterns in turn are responsible for the constantly evolving standards and their effect on those around us, including customers, suppliers, employees and shareholders that we deal with daily.

Business deals with more than just the physical realm. An awareness that understands that the cause or why of the physical environment is our desire patterns and their influence on the two building type blocks of the physical environment that include changing cycles and hierarchies will help a person begin to understand the origin of value. It is the nature of cycles and hierarchies that permits this physical world to manifest, to move from ideas to matter.

This awareness can move us to the next question. Who controls the effect of the actual physical manifestation of this world? Who is responsible for the ideas that start the "physicalization" of these ideas? Where do the ideas come from?

The answer in this creative exercise is that we do.

So how does this control manifest? As stated earlier, it is controlled by the ability of our super-conscious mind* activity. It is through this super-conscious mind activity that the physicalization process begins and manifests physical results.

So how does this super-conscious mind activity work? A definition and awareness of this concept as a root cause of how we are involved with the creative/creation process is as follows: There is a hierarchy of mind activity that pervades that with which we are involved. Just as we are aware that there are waves that permit the use of cellular phones despite the fact that the technology cannot be seen with the naked eye, so does this hierarchy of mind activity exist. Beginning with the innermost or highest level of mind or consciousness is where the super-conscious mind resides. Super-conscious mind activity has access to all of creation and its knowledge and awareness. Through creations interrelatedness as stated with the Buddhist tradition that everything is interrelated, the super conscious mind is responsible for what we experience within the desire patterns that arise in us all.

To expand on the attributes or abilities of the super-conscious mind: It has access to all knowledge and information on the physical, mental, emotional, psychological, psychic, and spiritual levels, and is responsible for all that manifests on those levels. It impacts the physical level, both direct and indirect. It has access to this knowledge and information through the simple act of knowing and its innate ability to attract that which it contemplates or desires.

There are many people today and within recent history who have demonstrated attributes of super-conscious mind activity. Edgar Cayce**, a Christian Sunday school teacher, used his ability within a sleep state over a period of 40 years to help and heal thousands of individuals with what seemed to be miraculous results.

Using the analogy of the cell phone, super-conscious mind activity can operate at the same digital frequency that permits that technology to tie the phones together. As one acquaintance states simply, "it's a miracle" when the switch is turned on and the words come from nowhere to go out in all directions to seemingly nowhere until attracted to the receiving unit of the cell phone with the right frequency into which we speak.

Chapter Summary:

Knowing how the super-conscious mind process works and being able to tap into it at will is another leadership skill that will be developed over the next 1,000 years by those who will lead.

As one focuses on the process of moving in the direction of a stronger understanding and insight into the natural laws that drive this physical reality, the vision that begins to manifest is what is called 180-degree vision. As part of that vision comes the understanding that we grow in awareness and vision by being involved in practical activities such as business and the value it creates.

Knowing that the super conscious mind exists through Awareness is a prerequisite of 180-degree vision. The ability to be involved but detached and to remain objective as to the outcome, is a prerequisite to remaining in that state called "living free" within the human condition.

CHAPTER
4

New Leadership Perspective –
The Personal Service Hierarchy

*Definitions, page 153

**Bibliography, page 193

***Root ideas, page 144

The ability to manage the Four Ss by integrating a company's strategy with evolving knowledge and information within the science, service, and spiritual arenas requires an expanded awareness of personal service. This is due in part to the point of difficulty and creative intensity and focus needed to expand a company's business model and strategy from a conceptual perspective or vision into a physical reality. When managing creative intensity within oneself and others, the focus of the individual's desire pattern is important and should be observed and understood over time.

Although service is one of the Four Ss defined within the book, based on today's focus on short-term financial and investment performance, it can be perceived as being impractical or counter intuitive to surviving in today's competitive environment. Most important is an understanding of the impact our perception of personal service has as a "root cause"* of ethics, behavior and the creation/creative process responsible for applying this knowledge and information into our business models.

The act of expanding our personal service perspective has much to do with evolving our awareness and frame of reference of what that idea or concept is and determining where we function from moment to moment within our decision process. It should also be understood that it is difficult to change the decision process and resulting behavior without a change in awareness. When our awareness evolves through expanded knowledge and information, our decision process and behavior change automatically without effort.

This would suggest that it is important to focus and contemplate the powerful impact awareness has on vision and our ability to function within a leadership role. This idea of automatic change in behavior is identified within many books and studies devoted to understanding the human condition and how we function within that human condition from both a positive and negative perspective.

Eckert Tolle in his book *The Power of Now* ** suggests that when awareness changes, behavior will change also. This idea is also found within the writings of individuals such as the late Father Anthony DeMello **, a Jesuit priest born and raised in India who wrote and lectured to the church's clergy on theological issues and topics that included an understanding of and insight into true awareness and how to impact it accordingly. Based on his experiences, Father DeMello was adamant within his teachings that behavior changes automatically when true awareness changes or is impacted.

What does this mean from a leadership or business perspective? For example, it is common when an individual within a leadership role has adopted a primary mode of behavior (as described within the leadership hierarchy in chapter 5) of using negative emotions through temper/anger outbursts (even if that behavior manifests sporadically for brief periods of time) due to learned behavior from past experience and a belief that it is necessary to use fear to control employee behaviors. Unless he/she discovers that until a large "A" change in awareness is arrived at regarding anger and its negative impact on the creative/creation process in others, he/she will probably spend an entire career cycle managing an organization with a very narrow leadership approach. In addition, he/she will attract others of like awareness and resulting frames of references.

That individual's frame of reference or vision will lead to the belief that anger and those negatives attributes and the display of those negative attributes are appropriate due to the physical environment as he/she perceives (e.g., "the end justifies the required behavior"). This belief will also have a propensity to make him/her believe that the above behavior in the form of temper/anger tantrums is due to external factors rather than individual conscious mind activity and the process by which the conscious mind reasons and establishes acceptable outcomes. That reasoning results in a very narrow definition of appropriate or correct behavior within the standards he/she has set and is constantly modifying for him/her and others. This activity also leads to enhancing confusion for those around them who are also escalating these negative emotions as part of the normal cycles within emotions.

Having observed the above behavior over the last 30 years as more the rule than exception within leadership behavior, what is the principle change in business theory and practice that will evolve over the next 1,000 years, especially as it relates to a more positive, creative style and an enhanced personal service perspective within leadership ranks? I believe it will be a leadership style or personal service perspective that jump starts a positive risk-free creative/creation process for all behavior within a company and will be the result of expanding knowledge within the four S's. The accomplishment of that enhanced leadership process will begin a cause and effect decision chain that creates a powerful new environment within the company.

A leader in this new millennium will have the skill set to identify the level of this awareness or personal service perspective objectively within themselves and others.

How does one gain awareness of the personal service perspective? An initial look at what motivates us to take action can take on a duality or opposite extreme — what I have dubbed in chapter 3 as a 180-degree perspective.

At one extreme are actions, which are purely self-serving. A manifestation of this behavior is the perspective found in many who lead today. It would be suggested that for one to benefit, another must suffer a loss (the roots of which are founded on a negative or limited capacity for this physical world to provide for us).

The other extreme can be found when a leader functions from a perspective where actions are motivated and decisions are driven primarily for the sole purpose of being of service to someone or some group (i.e., customers, employees, shareholders or other constituents).

A hierarchy can be constructed within any part of the personal service hierarchy (page 91), as well as on either end of the spectrum within the hierarchy. An example within the hierarchy of being of service to someone is the highest level of service or what could be considered to be the most extreme and most effective perspective. It can be defined as service or action that is manifested from a desire pattern that has been labeled "unconditional love" (page 91).

Although there are many definitions for unconditional love, the definition I use within the personal service hierarchy is those thoughts and behavior driven by both a caring and nurturing perspective that does not seek to benefit directly or indirectly from a decision to take an action. This includes benefits from the leader's standpoint that are both an internal (emotional) benefit, an example being that we give or perform a service because it makes us feel good or external (physical) benefit, i.e., we give because we will receive back tenfold to the decision-maker when an action or decision is made.

An understanding and awareness of this personal service hierarchy or building block of desire patterns for all value that is created within a business environment results in a person being in a position to tie into a higher level or focus on those root causes of how and why value is created. The higher a leader functions in understanding this creative process, the more successful that person will be consciously with tying together those desire patterns for customers, employees and shareholders. The effectiveness of our creative process grows exponentially as we begin to analyze our motives and those subtle motives (ulterior motives or rationalized and unconscious motives). The simple question "Why am I so moved to make the company perform at an even higher level?" is ingrained in us and should give us insight. We also should ask who benefits and who loses, and how long term or short term is the benefit.

The importance of moving from whatever level drives us currently to the highest level within this model will have a powerful impact on our career success and the emotion attached to the total career cycle, as well as what we define as success and failure. Understanding a movement up the hierarchy is important as one major objective of the book, which has been to increase the quality of life within those people reading, and those people impacted by the thoughts and ideas presented. This objective was also stated as one of the original subtitles of this book, which was "surviving a successful career".

It is suggested that unless one moves away from egocentric motivation for decisions and behavior, each of us who participate in leadership positions will be destined to grieve significantly (whether we choose to acknowledge it or discern it consciously) during most of our careers as we justify behaviors and performances that we define as success. This will be especially true during the latter part of our careers and lives, as we become more anchored in our conscious mind perception of reality that is driven by an egocentric thought process.

At its purest form, a person anchored in the highest level of personal service will automatically function without effort from a perspective that the sole purpose of his or her role in leadership is the act of being of service to everyone with whom he or she comes in contact, both directly and indirectly.

A person's service perspective can be discerned by observing how he or she functions on a daily basis, especially within emotionally driven situations, and spontaneously in both words and resulting deeds. One might see right away that the knowledge, skill set and discernment needed to observe objectively without judging would place issues of trust and caring on a whole new level of awareness.

Add to that our understanding of this physical environment along with its constant motion and changing cycles and hierarchies and our "point of view" would have us functioning from the highest level within the management hierarchy (found within chapter 6, page 117), "awareness through awareness".

The premise behind the personal service hierarchy and the cycles within the hierarchy is simple. We are all subjected to the conscious mind's flow of thoughts moving back and forth in the assessment of situations from both positive and negative emotions as we perceive or define the causes of a situation or behavior.

This conscious mind's flow of thoughts is driven in part from within its attempt to discern the physical environment and to relate to its surroundings by the positive and negative tendencies or capabilities of our heart until we anchor in a higher level of awareness. This activity or assessment of the environment will move constantly between the two extremes (positive and negative) as we attempt to solve problems and creatively develop actions and responses in all areas of our lives, especially those within our business professions. It is important to evolve our ability to manage awareness through awareness to focus. This conscious mind activity.

What is especially important from a leadership standpoint is that we understand that we do attract people of like personal service hierarchies around us, and they will be a driving force as to how the company focuses and on what — and on whether the company grows, stagnates or cycles out of existence completely.

What is equally important from a leadership standpoint within this attracting capacity is that it can be considered to be a root cause of personal performance within the value creating process by all individuals the company touches. The level of our attracting capacity leads to increasing physical results and enhanced financial performance for employees, suppliers and owners, as well as enhanced value to clients.

This attracting process is truly a root cause of what is to follow within the company as leadership evolves in the direction of developing and implementing activities, systems, policies, and business models that drive its ethical perspective as well as the resulting transactions.

An example of this is if the company primarily focuses on issues important to the company, such as management systems that track financial results (or systems that manage results — found within the second level of the management hierarchy described in chapter six, page 117). There is then a powerful tendency to lose track of where the value originates as well as a loss in our ability to attract it. How can a company correct this loss of focus? They can focus on those issues that create growth and personal networks that facilitate and move clients along their own purchasing behavior hierarchies.

For example, a new millennium business model would be a proactive posture towards moving a client from purchasing decisions based principally on fear or driven from the need to gain and maintain control, to decisions that are motivated or driven by the client's change in awareness and the need to satisfy an expanding desire pattern through knowledge and information. In addition, we may move them on to decisions based on even higher levels of awareness. This would be evidenced by the desire and resulting purchasing pattern being driven from a perspective of empathy and caring for the people who provide service to them. A higher motivation from a client or buyer would be the desire to be of service to the person selling the product or service. Their purchasing decision would be impacted by the fact that they made the decision to buy value that has been created due in part to the evolving desire patterns of all individuals touched by the transaction. In other words, to be aware that we/they create value by purchasing or consuming (creating value both ways).

To restate the above, a person involved in developing or evolving an organization strategy must constantly focus on the cause of buyer needs rather than the value of bottom line enhancement.   At its core, the cause or control root cause are the needs of the person using the company's product or service. It is founded on the old adage that states: "if you focus on the needs of the client (while being aware of the impact on the revenue and expense stream), the profitability or result of that activity will take care of itself."

This is not to say that both clients and profitability activities should not be managed simultaneously, but rather that to handle the velocity of change today, a more intense focus on client above financial result is what is needed. That change requires a creative thought process that is functioning at a very high level. A high level of creativity is discerned when one can take the dream of an individual as found in the book *The Four Agreements* written by Don

Miguel Ruiz ** and creatively move it to "a dream of a city," or company in our case (also known provincially as an organization's formal and informal research and development effort). This focusing effort is truly a major responsibility of leadership and involves the process of influencing the desire and need patterns of others.

Included in the focusing effort described above is an understanding of where the industry is currently and in seeing the potential that can be offered at the next level of value as perceived by groups that use the company's value output.

What happens once the decision and resulting awareness culminates in a 180-degree change in perspective within that person looking to evolve his or her leadership focus? What replaces the original ego-based internal perspective (i.e., the company profitability)? The answers lie in management systems that focus on enhancing everyone's personal service cycles and hierarchies leading to a more ethical environment. The change and evolution of the company's model grows exponentially and the company is catapulted ahead within its total environment.

In summary, by focusing on the root causes found within this book, a leader will see a vision that can become a company dream that leads to exceptional levels of service and commitment to all the people it touches, both directly and indirectly.

The personal service hierarchy (combined with an un-understanding of all cycles and hierarchies found within this book) defines the alternative that one should focus upon to look to a higher level of service. It is how leaders can start to evolve, understand and focus on the people they are responsible for leading as they replace a purely mercenary perspective focused on results. This will be the vision of leadership in this new millennium.

Moving back to the personal service hierarchy, this hierarchy is applied by moving from tangible to intangible needs or desire patterns of individuals as clients, employees and shareholders. These levels include needs relating to the physical, mental, emotional, psychological, physic and spiritual needs that are both conscious (.0001 percent of total) and subconscious (.9999 percent of total) desire patterns within the human condition.

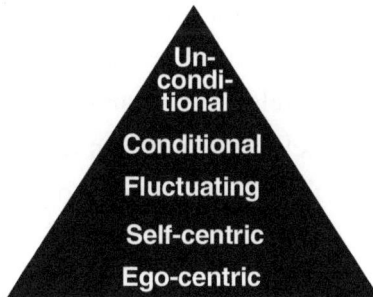

Exhibit 4.1
PERSONAL SERVICE HIERARCHY

Unconditional - The desire to be of service with no need for conscious or subconscious self-gratification. Benefiting from one's actions becomes incidental to root motivations.

Conditional - This level transitions from ego-based reasoning to reasoning and logic or justification that is predominantly based on issues of service as a standard for decisions and behavior. Unless a leader sees value added within an activity or process it is all but impossible for that person to incorporate it into their business model and environment.

Fluctuating - This level changes with the natural cycles of emotions and desire patterns, back and forth between ego* and ego-less reasons for decisions and behavior.

Self-centric - This level finds one's decision process primarily focused on issues of benefit to self and those that are immediate to one's awareness, such as family, employees, and friends.

Ego-centric - The root cause of this self-focus is due to an understanding that one is separate from all others and reflects a root cause perspective that there is an adversarial understanding of all relationships and motivations. As stated above, there is a belief that creation and the creative process is finite and that for one person to gain, another must suffer a loss.

An example of this finite idea is found within the investment community and its focus on short term and straight-line type financial performance and trading activity (although this behavior or logic can be found in all industries and walks of life). The historical focus by so many participants (company leadership, investment professionals, and investors) is a major cause of many companies' financial models due to myriad reasons that lead to performance standards that drive a company's limited culture and ethical perspective. Government regulations also impact significantly on leadership focus and are driven off a fluctuating level of awareness (lack of 180-degree vision) within those legislative and regulatory participants.

If this perspective seems to be the rule and not the exception, one can see how in the book *The Four Agreements* by Don Miguel Ruiz** that the dream of the investment community or regulatory process can truly become a nightmare.

Chapter Summary:

The motivating reason for behavior — be it how businesses sell products and services, why we employ ourselves and take direction, or how people lead others to perform creatively — will change from an ego-centric service perspective to an unconditional perspective as found within the personal service hierarchy (page 91). The negative emotions such as fear mentioned earlier as a motivator along with shame, grief, and the ability to condemn other people's actions through a narrow definition of correct behavior will decrease when moving people to action. These negative emotions as motivators will be replaced with positive emotions resulting in knowledge, information, and awareness being the primary motivators. It will be that positive feeling or motivation (empathy and love) that will become the driver or root cause of our expanded creation/creative capability that results in behavior driven by our desire to be of service to those around us unconditionally.

That evolving behavior above will also impact our behaviors both as consumers and family participants. For example, as participants in non-work related activities that reflect an evolving frame of reference, we will reflect a prosperity consciousness where we consume not only to fulfill our own desire patterns but to help others fulfill theirs as well.

It will be the above structural change in awareness* that will set the stage for all who focus on the issues developed within this book, either directly or through the focus of this new leadership awareness. It will be in this structural change in awareness that the groundwork for enhanced prosperity will grow exponentially. It is also where future business ethics will begin.

CHAPTER

5

The Leadership Hierarchy

*Definitions, page 153

**Bibliography, page 193

***Root ideas, page 144

As stated in prior chapters, our vision or understanding of our role as a leader is impacted almost completely by our awareness and understanding of life and the human condition. This awareness and vision is impacted through conscious mind activity and is a learned process. How broad or narrow this outlook may have become is based on the standards and values we have learned moment by moment throughout our lives. This vision and outlook drives our desire patterns and behavior from a hierarchy of emotions.

Chapter five presents a leadership hierarchy that helps readers analyze what might be driving their behavior from a root cause emotion perspective and what is driving their eventual decisions within each decision cycle*. It helps business participants by providing a framework that can be used to initiate an objective assessment process within them and others as to what is moving them and what is focusing their attention.

It can be used to help us observe our conscious mind activity that is driven by the natural cycles as a result of ongoing fluctuations between positive and negative emotions. When used in conjunction with the management hierarchy (chapter six, page 117), the leadership hierarchy is meant to summarize the root causes of activities we choose to carry out within our perceived responsibilities. It is where we actually spend our time within a leadership mode as a result of our dominant emotion or perspective. It is the root cause of our vision of what is happening around us and the root cause of our vision of how we as leaders attempt to tie in to the creative/creation process that results in value.

A 180-degree expression of these perceived responsibilities can be seen in how we spontaneously or unconsciously function. Do we see our primary responsibility within the leadership function as minimizing risks (real or perceived) at one end or maximizing individual creativity on the other end? This creation process eventually leads to tangible transactions and physical value. Our ability to assess and balance both ends of the spectrum is critical as we finalize our decisions and move into action.

The term "perceived responsibilities" points to one of the most difficult problems within leadership. Leaders should spend a majority of their time and focus in the development and implementation of their perceived responsibilities. Management systems should be set up and maintained to focus on accomplishing activities which support the creative/creation process in themselves and others.

The conscious and unconscious assessment of issues by individual leaders and the resulting decisions that flow from that assessment result in the positive and negative cycles that companies experience.

A company's changing performance cycles owe their root cause to individual leaders as they move through their individual awareness cycles. It is also from these individual awareness cycles that their decisions are shaped.

The word "unique" is used to describe a person's individual awareness cycles as they exist without trying to assess whether or not they should be considered to be positive or negative, competent or incompetent — whether they are or not from our own emotional standard or perspective. What is being suggested here is that the historical judgment of leadership behavior with a two-dimensional standard should fall by the wayside, when a multidimensional perspective replaces it, especially when an understanding of the multiple-directional nature of the physical and mental reality presented within the management hierarchy (chapter six, page 117) impacts the reader's awareness.

The diversity of issues within the management hierarchy areas of focus suggests that a decision impact at one level in the hierarchy might be considered correct, while the impact in another level would be considered wrong. Discussions with a two-dimensional determination of right or wrong are nonproductive. This is especially true in assessing our contribution as a leader who wishes to add ego-satisfying accolades or justification for his/her behavior.

The issues impacted by each decision and the cause and effect chain that follows from the multiple dimensions found within the management hierarchy (page 117) show that in the scheme of things decisions impact each level (e.g., activities, result, emotion) differently within the hierarchy. This is true when leaders are preoccupied with judging decisions or behavior as being positive or negative. Where and how will the assessment of decisions and leaders be judged in the future? The answer will change with awareness, such as when a leader sees with inner vision how an investment in his/her company's business model moves from a profitability and control focus with clients to a model that expands knowledge and information for clients.

At the center of the leadership hierarchy is a delineation of tendencies that shape behavior and range from our ability (or our heart's ability) to feel both positive and negative feelings that radiate from what is referred to as our feeling or emotional nature. In esoteric circles, it is these emotional capabilities that start the process by which we are involved in this physical world and which are the root causes of behavior.

An example of this two-dimensional vision can be articulated in what the Buddhists have called the eight negative abilities of the heart (the ability to feel hatred, shame, fear, grief, condemnation, race prejudice, pride of pedigree, and a narrow definition of appropriate behavior), and eight positive abilities or tendencies of the heart. All move us into action (e.g., the fear of losing our job or company due to its being purchased). These eight positive and negative abilities or capabilities of the heart can be seen within the leadership hierarchy as a root cause of behavior. These are also the root motivations that are part of the human condition that all of society creates for itself.

The root causes of behavior are a result of our ability to experience and feel positive and negative fluctuations in emotions tied to the input we receive from our senses. These emotions are part of conscious mind activity and process. It is our tendency to form opinions based on the five senses coupled with our cognitive skill level where we begin the action and reaction process by which we go about the leadership process. It is also here that we are part of the creation process.

The following hierarchy moves from negative to positive aspects or tendencies of emotion and influence our decisions directly:

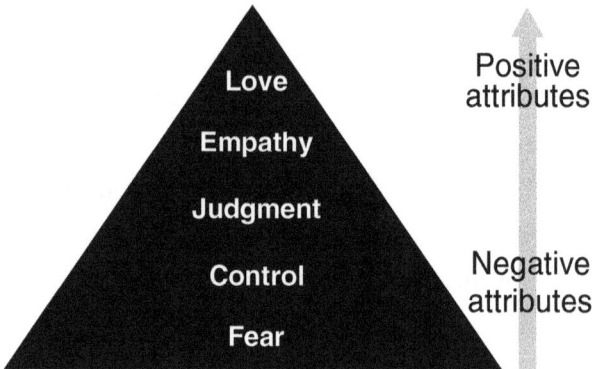

Figure 5.1
LEADERSHIP HIERARCHY

Love: The highest level within the hierarchy is a decision process shaped by an individual's ability to feel and see the environment as one. Where an understanding is gained that because of the basic building blocks of life and consciousness, all people are one and part of all that happens in this physical life. It is from this level of awareness that the Buddhists' statement "all things are interdependent" is a statement of physical reality.

It is understood when functioning from this high level of awareness that each of us has a universal impact on every other person and we are influenced by all who have existed, are existing and will exist in the future. It is with love, as defined in many circles as that which is universal and unconditional in nature, which drives a person's vision of this world. His/her decisions manifest from the highest frame of reference within the hierarchy and are filled with understanding and awareness. When tied to the management hierarchy (chapter six), that person is constantly managing awareness through awareness.

Empathy: The next level within the hierarchy deals with decisions that are dominated by empathy and understanding. It is here that the individual's service perspective leaves behind completely self-serving and ego-based behavior. He/she perceives that everyone is impacted by the actions he/she takes and he/she begins to eliminate the normal activity of judging behavior from a right/wrong perspective. That two-dimensional perspective becomes non- productive as part of decision activity.

Judgment: This level ties the positive and negative decision-making perspectives together, where an individual incorporates the provincial activity of judging environmental activity as right/wrong, good/bad and (usually in a business situation) legal and non-legal in nature. Decisions are based on man's law (legal system) or that which has been delineated within the legal arena. Moral judgments are also a part of assessing decisions based on appropriateness within an industry or business in general. Legal precedence preoccupies the decision process.

Control: A person preoccupied with defining and focusing leadership activities and decisions at the control level of the hierarchy will attempt to obtain and maintain control of as many environmental components as possible within the disparate parts of an organization. A summary of those disparate parts as found within the strategic management process framework page entitled "The Optimum Service Organization."

It is at this level that participants mistake their ability to assess conscious mind issues and in turn develop the control points through formal business processes that begin to dominate employee activity and focus.

An example of this mentality is the statement, "If you cannot measure and track it, it cannot be managed." Each activity within an organization is driven by this mindset, from sales and sales management activity to planning and budgeting activity and methodology.

Fear: At the lowest level within the leadership hierarchy is what can be considered to be one of the most basic of human motivators and which drives significantly more activities within the business arena than even I once thought. It is ingrained in our understanding of behavior and is a powerful teacher of behavior at all ages and stages of our lives. It is here that industries evolved their models for motivating clients, employees, suppliers and shareholders. It is also here that we can begin to focus on the root cause of the thought process that is driven by natural issues of instinct that stimulates behavior. These instincts run from physiological to psychological requirements or needs.

Although the term root cause is used to define that which begins the process of thought, it should be noted that every cause or root cause can be considered to be the effect of a more intangible or abstract idea or cause. I use the term root cause more to define that point at which we can start to modify our thought or belief process based on our own awareness. This is important in order to evolve our own decision system and to personally drive our ethics framework.

This personal ethics framework should evolve as it becomes based on more universal ideas and understanding that are in line with an expanding awareness for all people touched by our business activity and decisions. As posed in the beginning of this book, where does the new "ethics begin"? It begins within each of us who leads.

A classic movie example of our impact through awareness we may have concerning the above can be equated to the ideas presented in the classic movie "It's a Wonderful Life" with James Stewart. Awareness grows when he is shown the potential impact of his behavior or alternative behavior as well as the alternatives to not only his life but also his decisions and what manifests from them. In the end, he transcends the feeling of fear and judgment experienced by most as a result of the negative side of the human condition in which we find ourselves participating.

103

Assessment of good or bad management activity is unproductive. When any time is spent justifying or rationalizing the quality of our decisions (or in taking responsibility for the positive results and/or affixing non-personal blame for negative results), nothing more results than the ego sense justifying its separateness from other individuals that we touch within the leadership arena. It will be discerned in the future as truly an activity that is deadly to the creative/creation process. It will be understood that leaders who demonstrate the above will be revealing that their egoic minds (definitions, page 167) are out of control.

A series of questions that the reader could ask himself/herself at this time might be as follows: Where do I focus the majority of time? At what level within the leadership hierarchy do I function when left to my own desire patterns? At what level do I make final decisions leading to company activities? And most important, from what level do decisions evolve when placed under pressure driven by fear, anxiety and limitation? How do I go about dispelling those negative attributes?

Answers are not important at this time — just the awareness that the above answers do define our understanding of what is happening around us as part of our frame of reference as referred to within the Stephen Covey ** example summarized within this book.

Chapter Summary:

Our leadership decisions flow from our assessment of what is happening around us and our desire to manifest value and results. What is actually created is a result of how we motivate others within the creative/creation process.

The leadership hierarchy shows the different perspectives that can influence our activity and focus as leaders. It shows how subtle ideas can result in the development of an environment where managing components within the management hierarchy (page 117) will result in significantly different results within everyone who is touched by the value that is created or not. The hierarchy moves from a predominance of using the negative attributes such as fear as a motivator to the use of positive attributes such as love and its impact as a motivator on the creative/creation process.

Based on where we are focused within the leadership hierarchy, we as leaders do attract others of like attitudes and vision, leading to what manifests physically within the business activity in which we participate. As individuals within a business process, we as leaders are responsible for such subtle aspects as the intensity of the attracting process within a company's situation to the quality of life experienced by everyone including clients, employees, suppliers and shareholders.

Question: So what is the objective of evolving leadership theory and practice over the next 1,000 years?

Answer: To have those who participate in the creative and creation process physically create in abundance all that we desire to experience — to live in a world of plenty where all people benefit directly as a result of their individual desire patterns and awareness.

This vision is what the evolving leadership theory and focus will realize over the next 1,000 years.

CHAPTER

6

The Management Hierarchy

Leaders that begin to see with 180-degree vision as a result of increasing awareness will realize a powerful change in experience and success. They will intuitively focus on longer term issues that impact clients, employees, suppliers and shareholders more profoundly over a more sustained period of time. The quality of life within the work environment increases significantly driving a higher level of creativity and value. Managing awareness through awareness becomes the natural focus with little or no effort. Creating an ethical environment for everyone touched by the organization is developed and maintained through balanced leadership and creativity. The management hierarchy in this chapter helps us rethink our current focus and how our activities and decisions are impacting the value creating process on all levels within the hierarchy.

This chapter presents the management hierarchy that will influence the awareness of choices we make and the multiple areas and activities they impact as a result of our decisions. This is especially true within the development of a management ethic, management systems, and culture. All areas within the Management Hierarchy (page 117) and Strategic Management Process summarized within the diagram "The Optimum Service Organization" in chapter two are influenced by a critical factor: the evolution of our awareness and frame of reference and the impact that evolution has on our decisions. It should also help us to understand the importance expanding awareness has in the efficiency and focus within the creative/creation leadership process.

An important point to emphasize again when looking at any idea, even a religious or spiritual idea such as the Buddhists' statement on interrelatedness is the difference between realizing interrelatedness and truly realizing interrelatedness. The first realization can be considered to be intellectual in nature or a small "r" realization of interrelatedness. The second type realization or large "R" realization impacts behavior that is 180 degrees in nature.

How can one see the difference? The answer is always through a change in large "A" awareness where behavior, as a result of this awareness change, happens without effort and where new desire patterns evolve within this behavior.

An example of the above applied to the reading of this book can be represented by how each of us responds to what ideas are being communicated. Unless one is at a point that requires an immediate change due to the environment one is in, a change in awareness and behavior will probably not occur at once. Those who have come to a realization that their belief systems concerning either their professional careers or private lives have not generated the results they had expected or hoped for may look closely at what has been said within the book and experience change automatically.

The management hierarchy presented here also helps expand our roles as managers, problem solvers, motivators and leaders. As one contemplates the extensiveness of the knowledge network needed (a spectrum of information stretching from Deepak Chopra and his work in quantum physics, to Stephen Covey and his study of human behavior and that which impacts our individual and group frame of reference*) to define the impact a decision truly has on the chain of events that follow, awareness should begin to form that results in the understanding that much of the decision process is completed within both subconscious and super-conscious mind* levels. Conscious mind activity and our behavior from that source are driven by reaction and not pro-action as we might believe within the creative process.

It should also become more apparent with large "A" awareness that super-conscious and subconscious mind activity is driven or focused spontaneously by the most intense and emotional desire patterns as a result of learned conscious mind activity. It is this focusing process that results in learning within the human condition through trial and error.

Super-conscious mind activity is much like a massive computer program that responds to a single keystroke on a personal computer. In this analogy, conscious mind activity is represented by the single keystroke with super-conscious mind as the massive computer program responsible for the impact on that which becomes physical. This analogy also represents the role the super-conscious mind has in the natural creative/creation process.

It is also suggested that current conscious mind leadership behavior and understanding, much like the computer key stroke that starts a chain reaction of programming causes and effects, has no awareness of the impact it has on that which is physically created. This is in part due to the fact that we lack the awareness of how we are part of the creation process.

The importance of managing emotion has been an emerging component understood by a number of prominent business consultants and educators today. These individuals have been on the leading edge of evolving leadership focus and are recognized for their ability to impact business leaders' ability to generate a heightened level of creative emotion within individuals. An example of this focus can be seen most in the book *The Work Matters* by Tom Peters **, also author of the previous bestseller *In Search of Excellence*.

In addition, an understanding that the creative/creation process automatically sets up what-if environments to focus and satisfy desire patterns in each of us as business leaders, participants and consumers should impact our insight into the role emotion has on resulting behavior and decisions on either side of a transaction (buyer and seller).

The question that should be constantly posed within leadership activity that manages emotion is: What is my current understanding of the creative/creation process and how does it impact the emotions of those we manage? This review should be repeated where consideration is given to all disparate parts or issues within the strategic management process (chapter two, pages 56 and 57).

For example, when focusing on the impact a marketing and cultural model or strategy might have on clients within the financial services industry, the questions might be asked: "How can I develop a service or information that would result in clients understanding their financial situations in such a way that would eliminate the fear that drives them within their financial decision process? What pieces of information would they need? I would truly like to be part of that activity that eliminates fear and increases their quality of life."

To restate the above example and to expand it to include other business participants' conscious mind activity and awareness might result in the following questions: "What is being developed within the above vision and how do I participate within the creative/creation process in order to create higher value for those around me, as well as myself?"

Or, "How do I help the leader or supervisor move that idea or dream from a personal perspective to a group or organization dream? How do I become part of this idea as a root cause for my future decision-making?"

And when assessing clients' needs and desire patterns, "What do I have to physically create to minimize physical, mental, emotional, psychological and other fears and/or respective desires to maintain their health and well being?"

The management hierarchy reflects the general areas (levels) that are impacted by every decision made, and helps define what drives an organization's management group when discussing culture, objectives, or management processes that focus frontline participants' energy and time.

Important questions to ask when looking at how we are focusing frontline participants might be, "How much of the frontline participant energy and time is for the convenience of the management group? How is the simple directive of 'staying within budget' impacting participants' time? Does the process facilitate or complicate that physical result. What is and is not getting accomplished and what is the resulting impact on value overall?"

Where organizations lose their efficiency and effectiveness during a period of extended cause and effect decision chains is in not understanding how much time is taken up with systems that attempt to control outcomes that do not impact risks or create value.

The management hierarchy at its lowest level starts with those activities that seem to impact more tangible components of the company. These are components that can be perceived and measured by the five senses. The management hierarchy then moves through a spectrum of increasingly more intangible ideas that are best managed through knowledge, information and awareness.

The management hierarchy and the ideas within it are awareness* enhancing tools. The components are root causes of what becomes physical. An additional root cause is the knowledge and understanding of what a comprehensive definition is for the spiritual component of the four "Ss". To repeat in a simplified definition, the expanded

113

spiritual component within the four "Ss" can be summarized as stated earlier in the book as an understanding of the physicalization* of ideas into matter, and not as a particular religious or theological perception or belief. What has just been suggested or discussed within this paragraph are but two of the 22 root ideas*** that will impact a reader's perception, frame of reference and resulting behavior almost automatically if the ideas within this document are contemplated and understood with large "A" awareness.

What can make the management hierarchy an even more powerful tool is to integrate it with the personal service hierarchy (page 91). What happens within a business activity when one begins to use the model either consciously or unconsciously? An example within the management and leadership of research and development would be the gap between what actually is important to consumers and what seems important from the organization's perspective narrows and much of the risk of product and service enhancements is reduced. This increases the results of the creative effort significantly, as well as enhances the efficiency and cost of the creative effort by minimizing wasted time and money within formal research and development efforts. This is especially true if the motivation for research and development historically has been driven off the two dimensional company focus (page 129) and perspective.

The management hierarchy can be used to facilitate or evolve the conscious mind focus to evolve problem solving activity and our eventual decisions. A possible line of self-inquiries that forms the groundwork for product/service development activities might be as follows: "How will what I currently believe to be the impact from a major decision result in balanced value creation? How will the different components or levels within the management hierarchy be impacted? How are participants impacted from a macro (group) and micro (individual) perspective? How will a decision or direction impact trends on the physical, mental, emotional and psychological levels in which we exist relate to buying and desire patterns we serve?" (Again, I want to emphasize that it is not important to have answers to the preceding question, but rather to focus the creation process beyond conscious mind activity to start that massive computer program analogy as discussed on page 117.)

All of these questions should be just the beginning and can be at odds with the common motivation for product development, such as how we can make more money from our customers and non-customers alike. This is not to say that the above question is improper, but rather it should be balanced after the initial questions are asked in order to bridge the gap between the needs of the company and client. Let it also be understood that the more-money-objective can be responsible for focusing activity and development without the correct desire patterns of clients and broaden the gap between successful and unsuccessful development.

The impact on the focus of research and development questions stated above must also be assessed from a perspective of how desire patterns within clients will evolve over time. This evolution should start with an understanding concerning the impact from a short and long-term perspective on behavior changes. This is especially true when one realizes that regarding the development of products and services, it is important to remember one vital truism: "Right product, right place, right price, right time."

Sadly, the reality often is "Right product, right place, right price, wrong time".

The impact or objective of expanding product and service offerings must also include a vision of how that result will increase value within its limitless dimensions. How will the decision being entertained impact awareness of the people served and how will it evolve their feeling of well-being?

When a leader is able to assess all the components found within the strategic management process (pages 56 and 57), the personal service hierarchy (page 91), the leadership hierarchy (page 100), the management hierarchy (page 117), and the knowledge hierarchy (page 124) and integrate those components simultaneously, all risk within research and development is eliminated. This skill is one that will evolve significantly over the next 1,000 years.

Figure 6.1 (page 117) illustrates seven levels of management focus that should be balanced in an individual or organization as they go about the decision process.

Note: Both group or macro management and individual or micro management decisions are impacted by the area in which a leader is focused. That focus in responsible for what drives and attracts others, such that with the thousands of decisions made within an organization on a daily basis, a culture is automatically established, and which in turn drives the ethics and behavior of a company over time.

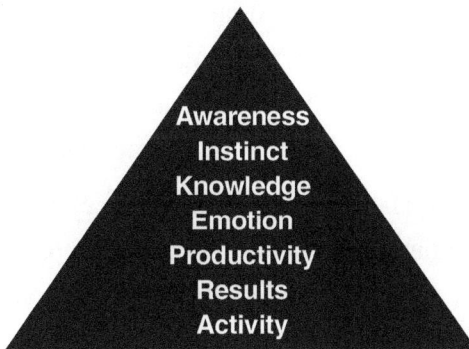

Awareness
Instinct
Knowledge
Emotion
Productivity
Results
Activity

Figure 6.1
MANAGEMENT HIERARCHY

Awareness - At the highest level of the hierarchy is the knowledge and information that helps us see the reality of our surroundings on both a physical and nonphysical level.

The ideas within this book are meant to expand and focus our understanding and insight into this idea of awareness and to begin a new dialog on these issues of awareness. The awareness that dawns automatically enhances our ability and insight into people and how they function.

The information network driven off of this awareness results in our ability to leverage creative consciousness into a focused desire to create value for ourselves and the business organization we are responsible for leading. We attract people, both employees and customers that reflect that heightened level of awareness (Note: This can be considered a natural law of attraction). A number of business theorists and practitioners have written on the topic of awareness. The most thorough treatment was completed by Fr. Anthony de Mello, S.J.** in his books and seminars on awareness, although the list of authors and teachers cited in chapter seven add insight into awareness as an idea.

Instinct - There are a number of factors important in understanding when people function most effectively and efficiently. An understanding that helps the conscious mind focus on those pieces of the puzzle that are responsible for behavior and skills include an understanding of instinct and the role that the conative portion of brain plays within an individual's blueprint as a root cause* of desire patterns within instinct. When we talk about "instinct" we use the word to describe basic desire patterns.

Tools dealing with this powerful component (or piece of our individual puzzle) have been described by a number of organizations led by the methodology as laid out by Kathy Kolbe**, CEO and founder of the Kolbe Corporation, in Scottsdale, Arizona. At the core of that methodology is a model that helps one focus on that aspect that helps to manage creative desire patterns. These desire patterns or abilities include the desire to observe, pattern, generate ideas, and physically demonstrate.

Within the conative profile provided by the Kolbe Corporation is an in-depth understanding of the intensity of our willingness and desire to create.

The development of a methodology to classify human instincts (as an addition to the development of testing and theories for measuring levels of intelligence and behavior or emotional patterns) is quite recent and has been developed over the last three decades.

Developed and simplified into a format that has become a powerful management tool is the treatment of the topic by Kathy Kolbe. It is the expansion within this type of knowledge and information that will help to drive components that bridge the gap in awareness and which focus the leader on understanding that piece of the creative or creation puzzle. Conation* as a piece of the behavior puzzle helps to expand our understanding of the magnitude of diversity within just the natural ability and desire of individuals to focus their creativity accordingly.

Knowledge - At this point in time, how well we process information and where we make and compare that information is at the center of understanding how to manage the knowledge base within ourselves, employees, and the customers for whom we are responsible for creating value.

Where is the management of knowledge going over the next 1,000 years? As stated in this book repeatedly, all of the physical, mental, emotional, psychological, psychic and other aspects of the reality we find ourselves participating within are subject to cycles and hierarchies.

These cycles and hierarchies include knowledge and information by which we go about the creative or creation process. Beginning with the thought process within an individual, expanding knowledge and information moves through cause and effect chains. Based on the decisions of that individual as successive cause and effect chains are developed, and in building on the knowledge that comes out of these decisions an individual impacts their company. Over time and success that company impacts an industry. This learning process within creativity when applied to business will result in quantum leaps in the ability to satisfy desire patterns and evolving needs for all business participants.

As this knowledge and information becomes physicalized, this creation idea or dream becomes accepted by industries as a new level within the industries group-dream of how an industry performs and creates value. Again, at a point when the industry accepts the physicalized idea, the industry comes to a point that builds that idea into that group's (the financial industry group in the example that follows) dream, idea and physical result. It becomes the next level within the industry's service or product capacity.

An example of this new idea applied to the financial services industry is when a breakthrough idea occurs as to how the industry communicates and moves people to transact their financial responsibilities from the significant use of fear to the elimination of fear within their business models. The old business principle "let the buyer beware" is falling by the wayside within most industries, at least from a legal standpoint.

Leadership in the current environment should include the learned knowledge that goes into creating every factor within their business model as well as the limitations known within their industry today. An understanding of the source and reason for the rules and regulations within an industry, and what results in transactions that create value based on these rules and regulations, must be grasped to drive change and evolution within that industry. Regardless of whether this knowledge and information is conscious or subconscious in nature, the need for it to exist is mandatory within the creative/creation process.

The management of the knowledge area of the hierarchy includes the importance of expanding and simplifying our understanding of knowledge within a more comprehensive model. This understanding must expand beyond just the testing for the level of efficiency and effectiveness (IQ tests) by which conscious mind activity retrieves input from the five senses and stores, classifies, and retrieves those points of knowledge.

An insight into a more comprehensive understanding of knowledge includes the awareness of its source as well. The source of this knowledge ties into the mental activity normally equated with conscious mind memory. The understanding of source should also impact our awareness as to the source of non-conscious mind activity. This would include the ability of that which has been called subconscious capabilities and the ability that comes to the behavior of a person who gains access to this information, as a result of hypnosis. The ability of the subconscious mind is demonstrated when one under hypnosis is asked to remember an event that was experienced, and specific details are recalled to an amazing degree. It has also been shown that behavior can be influenced dramatically by the behavior demonstrated by people under hypnosis who believe themselves to be something other than what they are.

This capacity is all but impossible for the conscious mind to accept within normal menial activity.

More important is the impact the super-conscious mind* has on those ideas that seem to flow randomly in and out of the conscious mind activity. Where is its source and what role does it have in the creative/creation activity?

As one moves forward in awareness and understanding of the idea of super-conscious mind activity, one realizes that the perception of having conscious and articulated control ends abruptly. All one has to do is ask a few simple question about the future flow of conscious mind activity and their ability to control thoughts they will be thinking just ten seconds from now. In other words, where will our conscious flow of thoughts take us and how can we think we are in complete control of that which happens if we cannot anticipate our conscious thoughts over the next ten seconds?

Another simple hierarchy that has been used to define knowledge as a focusing tool is the impact awareness has on what a person knows and how they demonstrate their level of knowledge and knowing. The knowledge hierarchy helps us to understand the level of knowing both within a macro situation (i.e., an industry's culture) to micro situations (i.e., what a person knows, based on how they behave). The hierarchy has four levels that move from not knowing to knowing as follows:

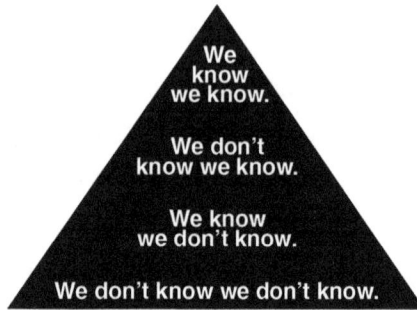

Figure 6.2
KNOWLEDGE HIERARCHY

In summary, the knowledge level of the management hierarchy is meant to impact awareness and to evolve our understanding of what is seen by the leader as he or she tries to respond to the environment being observed. It should also begin to humble the leader who realizes that any notion of seeing that which is real in terms of the creative/creation process is more out of his or her conscious mind control than within it.

In turn, that which really manifests is the result of a plan that is integrated with us all and evolves from the conscious, subconscious and super-conscious mind activity and desire patterns in each and every one of us. A perception by a leader who entertains any other notion (like taking credit for a company's result) is like sitting next to the river and paddling the water downstream — and feeling self-satisfied by all the activity. When functioning from a control level in the management hierarchy, a leader would find himself/herself taking credit for the flow of the water.

Emotion - At the center of behavior is the ability of the body to control and regulate its physical characteristics through the use of the five senses, and is tied to learned knowledge and past experiences as a result of the five senses. The body and mind relationship results in an integrated response to the physical environment in which we function and which dictates when action is required. This action is precipitated by the impact emotion has on the chemical integrity and stimuli to the nerve, circulatory and muscular systems. Simply put, conditional and unconditional responses both physically and mentally provide much of the human condition under which we live and from where we grow in awareness of our environment on the many different levels we function within. Emotion (integrated with all other aspects within this management hierarchy) is at the base of what moves us into action and which places us in a position to participate in the physical creative/creation process.

It is within our emotions (as effect) that we spontaneously run through our process of logic by which we arrive at our final decisions and move within the creation/creative process. It is also within this activity that we attract to ourselves the environment required to fulfill the desire patterns innate in all of us. People, places and generalized events place us in a cycle and resulting hierarchy of issues and ideas that must be satisfied as we move through this life cycle to which we are all so consciously attached.

As stated early in this chapter — from issues of principled leadership as defined by Stephen R. Covey**, and the focus on emotion, as described by Tom Peters** in his book *The Work Matters* – a more comprehensive understanding of emotion and the role it plays in the creative/creation process will be at the center of leadership evolution over the next one thousand years.

Productivity – Leadership's focus on productivity is the next level of the hierarchy and addresses an individual leader, within an organization or industry that defines their activity by that which is being physically managed. This physical focus is usually preoccupied with those ideas and components or outputs that preoccupied leadership over the last 100 years, starting with the work by Frederick Taylor.

It is driven off the requirement to quantify ideas or intangibles into a production or activity result. It is also driven significantly from a numbers orientation, and is predominantly a financial and accounting vision of the company and its environment by the leaders and managers within that company.

The root cause of this focus on activity is a result of the information and training in which so many of the business leaders responsible for leading today's companies were schooled. Individuals are taught the correct methods of thinking within most institutions of higher learning (lawyers are taught to think like lawyers, financial people are taught to think like financial people, medical doctors are taught to think like medical doctors).

This learned thought process within formal education evolved with its origin in the scientific method of problem-solving (the study of "that" which is physical and the processes permitting "that" in its physicalization process) and was applied to the business and business education arena. In particular, the scientific method of problem solving was employed when the business arena began to expand its formal process within the business education arena in the form of developing theories and tools that lead to what is perceived as the focus of business — that of creating a financial result as a result of a physical result.

Applied, this financial thought process or approach seeks to define a revenue stream and to impact that revenue stream by increasing revenues (so many times through price increases) or decreasing expenses (cost cutting) within a short term or annual perspective. This result is due to the short-term focus of financial information as part of the cycle of business. This process is also established through accounting and financial theory, training, and recording convenience.

It is legitimized within accounting principles that are biased towards managing hard dollar income and expense statement line items. This process has a tendency or bias towards making commodities of costs and prices and minimizing soft dollar revenue (value) and costs (such as human relationships, knowledge and information of participants, time and duration of relationships, and long term issues of productivity).

Discussions that concern themselves with issues such as investing in human capital are an attempt to quantify that very nebulous term within accounting and financial theory. In so many cases, discussions are based on much of the above but rarely is anything implemented due to our natural propensity to minimize risks and to handle disparate parts of the environment separately instead of simultaneously.

This is due to what we were taught influenced behavior as a root cause that leads to a blend of the theory X and Y management philosophy, and is reflected within the need to quantify productivity and results. This situation has been the focus in business theory over the final forty years of the last century.

The intensity of this focus on quantifying production activity that leads to financial results has been all-consuming and results in the tendency to create and develop faulty economies of scale, to establish a process and belief that a company is successful and controlled, and in restricting change — change that would involve risk due to the currently weak process by which we assess change. This would lead to a loss in the importance and strength of precedence coupled with risk aversion within a successful and controlled company perceived historically as the value created by leadership.

A summary of a few focusing topics regarding managing environmental issues that are applied by companies to the above quantification process is delineated in Table One below. It shows a 180-degree focus between disparate components of some of the issues within the Table entitled "Strategic Management Process", shown in chapter two.

Another way to define the reality of a company that has developed management systems that reflect a focus on productivity is found within the next management hierarchy component: control. It is a company that reflects a financial/organizational focus as opposed to client or creation/creative focus, and demonstrates the following activities:

Financial Focus		**Client Focus**
Planning company needs	O	Planning client needs
Managing hard dollars	O	Managing soft dollars
Short-term data base	O	Long term relationship database
Macro client data base	O	Micro client data base
Marketing: Company needs	O	Client needs focused

Control - Within this management focus, the vision of that person driven from a control perspective will be preoccupied with minimizing real and perceived risks. There is a tendency for that leadership person's vision to reflect that which finds its root cause as what has been coined the negative tendencies or abilities of the heart as defined within the leadership hierarchy in chapter five. These negative tendencies are part of the natural cycle found within the current human condition that is driven off of the nature of cycles, be they physical or mental (idea) cycles.

The leaders who find themselves within that mind set will discover that they will attract other individuals of like awareness to support their perspective and will be responsible for creating an environment that lacks confidence in the creative/creation process.

They will find that they lack the large "A" awareness as to the interrelatedness of everyone and everything, per the statement cited in the Introduction and derived from the Buddhist tradition. Due to their own belief system, they will perceive that we are all separate from each other (primarily due to the inability of the five physical senses to pick up our interrelatedness), whether conscious or not. A resulting belief is that this is a finite world with limitations, and that for one to benefit another must sacrifice.

One of the most devastating attributes of this mind set within a leadership person is the belief in an environment and reality that the ego sense* develops that anything that takes him or her away from a vision is due to other people and environmental issues. This idea also leads to an adversarial tone within their interactions with the people they lead and the clients they serve.

This posture is in many cases a result of the overriding belief that the conscious mind activity is all that is real when one processes information from the physical world around us. This simple misconception can change spontaneously when awareness expands.

It can be observed that rather than understand the inter-relatedness of all business conditions and creation as it follows a very natural creative/creation process, many people prefer to deal with disparate or different parts of the physical world separately.

For example, through thought, word, or deed they address the four Ss — strategy, science, spirituality and service — as independent subjects to be handled with different sets of rules, regulations and behaviors. For example, if one's family should be treated differently than other known people, who should be treated differently from people who are not known directly? (This insight as to how people respond became apparent in the wake of our experience of terror after September 11, 2001.)

Although the discussion might sound like one of condemnation, it would be unproductive to criticize a person lacking awareness into the interrelatedness of this physical world. Much of the reason for the apparent short sightedness comes from the ego sense or the belief that we are separate from each other and that our thoughts and situations are unique and end with our physical bodies and our personal thoughts.

All that is needed is an impact on large "A" awareness and the more comprehensive understanding of the creation process and our intimate role within that process becomes understood. An important point to understand here is that behavior can change spontaneously, an activity that is going on constantly in each of our lives at one point or another.

One of the main problems with the above lack in leadership awareness is that this results in a bias or tendency to judge behaviors within a narrow definition of what is appropriate or correct. Consequently, the abilities of others are viewed as shortsighted or incorrect.

There are a number of behavior characteristics of this leader that reduce decisions to issues of personal control. However, as one becomes aware of this management hierarchy, the ability to see a leadership process as the constant desire to develop systems that place the leader in control of more rather than less information is a common denominator.

The leader preoccupied with control has the misconception that it (control) can be obtained. He or she mistakes the flowing of the water downstream (the analogy used earlier) as a result of the paddling and believes that without the control of the paddle, the water (value creation) will stop. Although this is an extreme oversimplification of the ability and skill of those who find themselves in positions of authority, please let it serve to impact awareness within our own internal definition of correct leadership behavior.

Activity – The lowest level within the management hierarchy and one that preoccupies the majority of us employed within a leadership or employee mode is the process of managing activity. A more comprehensive definition of managing activity with a stronger understanding of the management hierarchy can impact awareness with the following expansion in the definition of management.

We can redefine all the positions of all of us who work to find ourselves in positions to create and manage value for others with every activity or transaction in business, and to consider ourselves as managers. The conclusion is that we all have an important role within the management process as participants.

This is suggested because when defining an activity, even the act of taking a pile of wood and locating it to another area can be described as managing that material flow. An additional example from the banking/ financial services arena is the role a bank teller has in dealing with customer transactions. At the core of a teller's position is the act of managing multiple transactions and the environment surrounding those transactions. If a teller attempts to handle a complete transaction without speaking a single word to that customer eliminating even the simplest of greetings, or chooses not to offer appropriate explanations to the customer when they are needed, the manner in which the money is handled becomes almost secondary. If a teller is not professional in the manner in which he or she builds customer confidence that the money is being handled properly, then the teller is managing that transaction to a worse outcome.

The point in awareness is that it should become apparent that everybody who works, no matter what their positions might be, should consider their activities as essential and themselves as managers. All people should be treated with respect and understanding, and receive added recognition for the quality with which they perform even the simplest of work activity.

For example, in the evolving understanding of ethics, as well as vision as focused on clients, all company models would change from ones that use fear and incomplete understanding and information for clients to models that move the client or clients to a new vision and awareness.

Chapter Summary

Within the human condition evolving desire patterns will be based on the elimination of what has been called the negative tendencies — abilities or emotions of the heart, and will be replaced with behavior and desire patterns motivated from the positive tendencies or abilities of the heart. The physical result will be a higher level of satisfied needs that will increase the rate at which new desire patterns are formed and satisfied within this new age of leadership, caring, nurturing, and skill. This will occur due to the focus and efficiency of leadership capabilities within the creative/creation process. It will result in an efficiency that anticipates desire patterns by clients in their idea state and would seem to be satisfied all but spontaneously.

The momentum of all these desire patterns as part of the cause and effect chain will grow exponentially and move from the idea or thought realm into physical manifestation in this physical world at a significant increase in ease and value.

Most important in the above designation of management would be the elimination of the classic differentiation between management and employees. This would be as a result of a new definition of value that would minimize or eliminate current hard dollar models of value. The current financial and accounting standards focus will be minimized over the next one thousand years. All of these results will be the effect of evolving leadership theory, understanding and awareness by those of us in leadership roles.

Note: For those leaders that take personal credit for that which has been created and who are not yet aware of just how little the ego sense has to do with creating the result from conscious mind activity (which is where the ego sense is developed with all its mistaken notions), it might be good to explore a more comprehensive understanding that the part we actually play in the creative or creation process is a humble one. It also might be a good time to reconsider the act of taking credit for a result.

As a leader within this new millennium, one should make sure that a transition is made over the leader's career cycle that encompasses a 180-degree change in awareness. In the case of an organization's life cycle, the change should be 360-degrees. The primary reason for a company's demise is failing to change from a focus on self to a focus on clients on a cyclical basis over time.

7

Changing Our "Frame of Reference"

I first heard of the idea of "frame of reference" when I attended a program presented by Stephen R. Covey, author of the book *Seven Activities of Highly Successful People*. In addition to discussing his perspective on corporate and leadership ethics, he explained and demonstrated his definition of frame of reference in part through his personal experience. This personal experience helped set the stage for a discussion on awareness of what the human condition is, how fluid it actually is, and how it can be changed with just one piece of information, moving to a significant and spontaneous understanding and change within his frame of reference.

Within this personal experience, he explained how with just one piece of information, we can change our whole idea or vision about a situation or event that is impacting us physically and emotionally. This change can result in how we judge. It can help us become aware of our natural tendency to offer up judgment on all activity and behavior around us based on our perception and vision of what is happening in this physical environment within a leadership, business or personal situation. Most important, this change in awareness can redefine our narrow definition of appropriate, one of eight negative tendencies/abilities of the heart (or feeling nature) (see chapter five, The Leadership Hierarchy) into a broader understanding of all that we see.

Within Covey's relating of his personal experience on a metropolitan train, he describes his level of discomfort with the behavior of a man and his three boys who entered a subway car where he and others were sitting. Upon entering the subway car, the man, who seemed to be in a drug induced stupor, did nothing as the three boys started to fight and throw paper at each other, finally hitting an elderly lady. Upon that event, Covey stated he approached the man, angered by his seemingly lack of appropriate parenting. The man, whose eyes teared up on his approach, apologized, stating he was having difficulty coping with the fact that he had just come from the hospital where his wife and the boys' mother had just passed away. He stated that he believed the boys were probably having trouble also but that he would try to calm them down.

At that point Covey indicated his whole way of feeling and his behavior changed as a result of his change in his frame of reference. The negative feeling or emotion turned to a positive feeling of empathy and concern.

Although this is just one event that probably lasted less than a few minutes, the point of the matter is that every moment within every waking hour of every day, we are bombarded with the flow of conscious mind thoughts and the resulting opinions flowing from those thoughts. This conscious mind activity within a leadership environment, as well as within the reality of the human condition we find ourselves participating in, is about our reaction to stimuli. Our reaction is a result of our hierarchy of knowledge and information acquired throughout our life and which we draw upon to make decisions and judge that environment. This activity begins at birth and continues through everything we do, say and learn, including our roles as leaders.

What is also important from a creative/creation process, is that the evolving frame of reference process above as "individualized" is responsible for that which happens within the physicalization of ideas into a physical result.

To use the Stephen R. Covey example to express even further the point of difficulty in defining that which is perceived through our vision (be it rose-colored or Pollyanna pink from a positive perspective, to dark brown from a negative perspective) and what is found more often than not in a business and leadership environment can be suggested as follows: What if Covey responded by saying that he did not care what the man and his sons had just been through with the death of his wife and their mother, that it was the man's responsibility to maintain his children's behavior in a public place (narrow definition of respectability)? Or, if he questioned whether the man was telling him the truth?

It is within the leadership decision process that much is discounted about what is true. In many cases, the discounting of truth is due to the leader's past experience with dishonesty within two-dimensional thinking where truth is perceived in absolute terms, such as in a court of law. In other cases, it is because that which is revealed suggests a decision or action that is not desired or which the point of difficulty or cost is too high to the leader. This is especially true if the leader's perception is anchored in a physical reality of limitation (found within the lower levels of the leadership and management hierarchies). This limited view or frame of reference can be considered the rule rather than the exception in what we believe or demonstrate within a leadership mode. It can be our predominant frame of reference within a business event or how we go about forming our day to day frame of reference.

The above example of discernment within the Covey story is also important in how we respond from a positive or negative perspective and its impact on the velocity of change, as well as one of the reasons the Buddhists are correct that "nothing is permanent, and all things are interrelated." It is that growth in knowledge and information within each individual person's frame of reference that has always driven the mass or collective frame of reference or perspective. The velocity of change has always been driven by the ability of the individual within his or her creative/creation capability and the desire to initiate, along with the ability to communicate this creativity and thought through both physical and nonphysical methods. Society has evolved over the last millennium based on the desire patterns and the individual's ability to collect and use knowledge and information as it arises from the individual's creative consciousness.

Much of this book has been devoted to developing new and expanding old theories, frameworks, concepts, vocabulary, and ideas concerning issues of awareness or vision. In fact, the idea to create this book came from the desire to seriously impact the quality of life for those who lead and the people they impact, both directly in the work environment as well as in their homes and personal lives.

Most importantly, it has been my intention to suggest a redefining of how we look at our roles and responsibilities as we progress in this new millennium — to focus on how we as leaders are responsible for the velocity of change and how to influence that change exponentially. To understand that we are but building upon all physical, mental, emotional, psychological, psychic and spiritual hierarchies that historically have moved and will move society in the future.

As our individual frames of reference change through this new knowledge and information, an example of which is how the four Ss (Strategy, Science, Spirituality, Service) should be and are integrated and impact upon themselves, our ability to deal with the creation of value and the creative thought process will expand whether we desire it or not. This expansion will be due to breakthroughs in everything from quantum physics (Deepak Chopra, page 205) and its role in our idea of how science and spirituality are integrated into the expansion of laws and protocol required of business leaders.

For example, within the breakthroughs in science it is being discovered within the realm of quantum physics that the light particles that make up the physical world (i.e., atoms and subatomic particles of light, which are at the center of science) find their origin in the void between those light particles that make up the physical world, as its basic building block. These building blocks are stimulated and react to the desire patterns of each of us (or what is now being called the spiritual aspect), just as scientists through the splitting of atoms are starting to realize that what they believe will happen influences the outcome within a scientific experiment.

Finally, there have been a number of authors referred to within this book. It is suggested that one of the two ways an individual interested in changing his or her frame of reference might pursue is the investigation of these authors' written material and programs.

The other way is by direct insight and sharpening our ability to know by knowing. This is accomplished by tapping into that source that originates within super-conscious mind activity, as explained earlier within the book. It is that source which has historically been referred to as intuitive or "gut feeling" by business participants. Honing that understanding of what that gut feeling really is and expanding our ability to understand when we have tapped into that creative force that has access to all knowledge and information on a higher level will be an evolving skill set of one who would lead. To develop that awareness or skill that is inherent to us as human beings, active participation within the creative/creation process should be a major personal objective.

143

To help facilitate the study of the individual sources used within this book, at least one page number has been added per author showing where the author was mentioned within the book and should not be considered complete, as each author's ideas have been cited throughout the book in order to demonstrate to the reader past precedence in many of these root causes and ideas. I should also point out that the topics covered are but an expansion in the hierarchy of knowledge relating to business theory and practice.

The 22 ideas/causes and recommended authors are as follows:

1. Awareness - Father Anthony DeMello: page 81; Pema Choldron : page 32

2. Base Needs - Abraham H. Maslow: page 9.

3. Conative Instinct - Kathy Kolbe: page 118.

4. Creative/Creation Process - Deepak Chopra: pages 62, 109, Esther and Jerry Hicks: page 45.

5. Cycles - Deepak Chopra: pages 62, 109; Dr. Kam Yuen: pages 63; Dr. Andrew Weil page 29.

6. Desire Patterns - Integrated Spiritual Traditions.

7. Ego Sense - Don Miguel Ruiz: pages 89, 93.

8. Emotion - Tom Peters: pages 111, 125.

9. Four Ss - Tom Franklin: page 40

10. Frame of Reference - Stephen R. Covey: pages 66, 109, 125.

11. Hierarchies - Abraham Maslow; Dr. Kam Yuen; Deepak Chopra: pages 62, 109.

12. Interdependence - David Pottrick and Terry Pierce: pages 9.

13. Interrelatedness - Dr. Kam Yuen: pages 17, 63.

14. Leadership Hierarchy - Thomas Franklin: page 100.

15. Law of Attraction - Esther and Jerry Hicks: page 45.

16. Management Hierarchy - Thomas Franklin: page 117.

17. Personal Service Hierarchy - Thomas Franklin: page 91.

18. Physicalization -Thomas Franklin: page 3.

19. Strategic Management Process - Thomas Franklin: pages 56, 57.

20. Super-conscious Mind - Thomas Franklin: page 170.

21. Vision - Eckart Tolle: page 32; John Naisbith: Appendix C page 187.

22. 180-Degree Management - Thomas Franklin: page 53.

As I stated in the forward of this book, I tried to keep the text short. This objective has been realized at the expense of including additional examples. The purpose in keeping the written material as brief as possible is due to my under-standing that in order for the reader to evolve his or her own frame of reference most effectively, he or she should "read less, contemplate more on his or her situation, and stay focused on the creative/creation thought process al-ways." I hope this has been accomplished.

This book has been about developing a new vision of what business can become from a more positive perspective or vision. We can be part of that positive vision as we turn within to evolve our thought process and redefine what our roles should be. By redefining their roles, leaders can increase the quality of life for themselves and everyone they touch in this new millennium.

Thank you for reading this book and I wish you much success, however you define it.

8

Student Supplemental Summary

*Definitions, page 153

**Bibliography, page 193

***Root ideas, page 144

This book was created to give you the opportunity to explore topics and issues you might not have had an occasion to consider. In particular, the book helps develop a stronger personal perspective and understanding of the role an individual can play regarding ethics and business. You will be guided to a better understanding of the motivation that is required in today's business arena and its constantly evolving ethical environment. The intensity of your motivation to succeed will greatly impact your perspective on ethics, and will help shape your career.

How self-motivated you are in acquiring information and awareness is a central focus of *Leadership: Where Business Ethics Begin*. Our ethical perspective is seriously impacted by our ability to maintain a high level of self-motivation. An indication of your level of self-motivation is whether or not you can do what has to be done to reach your objectives regardless of your immediate desire to do so. So what does that mean for you?

Simply KNOW that although the study of business theory and practice can be long and tedious, *it teaches the process to observe, understand and deal with your physical environment and the issues you face within a business/work environment.* KNOW that this process deals with many components which are presented in the schematics summary shown on pages 56 and 57, and explained throughout the book. KNOW that you will be working within that process throughout your life and career.

So what does this mean to you at this point? Understand that students are all in a position that works at odds with exerting the natural desire to express personal freedom. That desire for personal freedom is a powerful drive within each of us and can impact negatively on our ability to function when motivated incorrectly.

When examining the various classes offered by your school and what the goals for those classes are, you may be able to determine that it will not be until you are in your career that you will be able to perceive the "why" of what you are presently learning. How you approach what is being taught and your desire to embrace these concepts begins your thought processes that will influence how ethical or unethical an environment you create for yourself.

Another question you might ask yourself at this point is how you will participate within a company and what opportunities may exist for you? If your answer is you do not know, then you may recognize the need to trust others to teach you the skills needed to perform well within a company's setting. It has been said that formal education would be much easier if we could work for 30 years in business and then proceed with focusing on what we need to learn.

Once you are in your business career you will move forward with your own understanding of what will lead to your success. The quality of your life and your ultimate success will be determined by working in an ethical business environment. By reading this book you will help prepare yourself for the development of a more powerful perspective on identifying and creating a more ethical environment. Classes that delve into the formal issues of ethics should also be a key part of your education.

So how do you begin to expand your own personal perspective on ethical behavior and/or self-motivation in business? And how do you motivate yourself to focus on and absorb what is being presented in this book?

Please begin to review and digest the material in the book knowing that you are building on what you have experienced personally. Know that as you review the ideas in the book, your perspective on and judgment about what is being learned are also evolving. This perspective will include the broad spectrum of knowledge and information you have acquired from parents, instructors, fellow workers, family members, and friends.

Competition: From tying your shoes and learning your ABCs, there have been demands placed on you to learn new things. When you were young, people responsible for your supervision taught you how to think and what had to be learned. Competition was introduced early in your life, both at home and at school. The activity we considered play resulted in direct or indirect competition with others.

Success, acceptance, and feelings of self-worth are engrained in us at an early age and begin to act as motivation if we compete, especially if we are successful (sports, grades, class rank, etc.). The quality of our lives increases with positive results from competition.

This natural competition continues throughout our lives, and we become adept at functioning in a competitive environment to such a level that we seek to set ourselves up in such a competitive environment. In other words, we accept the idea of competition as a requirement for everyday life. In many cases, this competition becomes part of our relationship behavior within our family life, and among friends and our fellow employees. It can also impact our behavior with our company's customers.

It is important to be aware that in business as you grow, your personal freedom expands and with your success come additional responsibilities, both legal and professional. Success will help you continue to shape your ethical behavior and define what you will and will not do. What you will do if driven primarily by the need to compete is significantly different from what you will do if you operate from a perspective of being of service within the business environment, and promoting the value that service creates.

What you will come to understand eventually is that there is a **balancing** between the ability to function in a competitive environment and to be of service while successful — especially over an entire career. Very seldom does one find success over an entire career if one stays focused solely on competing. This is because there is a natural cycle to how we compete over time that manifests both positive and negative situations within the competitive environment with which we identify.

So how do you begin to move in the direction of guaranteeing your lifelong success?

Become aware and understand the concept of being of service by developing what is described in the book as 180-degree leadership vision.

So, where do you start?

Please think about the statements below and the ideas presented in the book. Choose to incorporate these concepts in your life.

1. Continue to learn how to compete, but within boundaries. Never lose sight of a principle goal in business of helping others by creating something of value and being of service.

2. Immerse yourself in acquiring knowledge and information from myriad sources. These sources can include your instructors, parents, relatives, friends and other co-workers and supervisors. Know that many times the information will be correct, but often it may be wrong. As you gain a greater perspective over time on the root causes of ethics, you will become better at discerning the difference.

3. Grow in the ability to view the environment from other individuals' perspectives and experience by staying anchored in a service concept. Know that sometimes within each of our conscious mind's flow of thoughts our thinking is correct about another's perspective. And, sometimes it is wrong and has no basis in fact.

4.   Know that the balancing of different aspects that a business faces is both difficult and critical from a competitive and service perspective.   It will lead to more ethical decisions that create better business environments.

5.   Acquire the ability to observe your emotions and thoughts and then detach from these emotions to begin to develop a truly objective perspective. The more you practice that decision process, the more observant and the less self -serving you will become. You will eventually obtain a highly ethical perspective.

6.   Finally, read through the book completely including the definitions and hierarchies. Then decide how you might proceed with the remaining portion of your educational career and motivate yourself to create an exceptional ethical perspective.

After finishing my formal education, I found a position in business that required me to deal with company issues similar to those described on pages 56 and 57. It became an important goal for me to positively impact the working environment and success of others. I have accomplished this by expanding my knowledge of business theory and practice, and most importantly by developing and applying inner intuition (that grows with time into higher states of awarness and consciousness). Listening to inner, clear states of awareness ensures appropriate ethics and right purpose are applied to all important decisions and actions. I found this process resulted in creating positive work environments.

I hope the same for you. Good luck!

Definitions

Awareness: The act of having or showing perception and knowing, as well as insight or vision. As used in the book, it is the perception and understanding of issues concerning how the physical realm develops and changes and how each of us are a part of that process moment by moment throughout our lives. An example of this is understanding how our super-conscious mind activity is in part responsible for the physical realm and is driven by our response to individual and group desire patterns. The evolution in our awareness can be considered a root cause that leads to an expanded business activity and the value it creates. (Page 8)

Business: Those activities which create something of value to individuals on at least one of the following levels: physical, mental, emotional, psychological, and psychic. The nature of business related activities result in the satisfaction of individual desire patterns that are the root cause of our hierarchy of needs as defined by Abraham Maslow**. Business is the term used to define the physicalization of ideas and concepts within the creative/creation process. (Page 19)

Business model: A constantly changing pattern for differing activities within a company's strategic definition of the value they are creating. It should also help to define how that value is distributed to differing participants. As an example it can be used as an imitation or emulation by employees within their own creative/creation process. The business model should provide the best possible exemplification either in physical reality (that which is provided) or in conception (that which is to be provided) and leads to a focus within the most important of statements within both formal and informal planning processes, the organization's Mission Statement. (Page 21)

Change: The term is used to define the movement and nature of the physical world as it evolves and impacts the human condition. The natural law of constant change is a root cause for all desire patterns and results in the need for the business function. From the most minute requirements of the cell and cell functions within the body and the needs that arise within those cycles to issues that equate to celestial realities of time and movement, all things are susceptible to the realities of ongoing change. This change is a building block of the physical world, as well as those idea and creative realms responsible for the physical world's manifestation. (Page 20, 36)

Conation: The mind has three aspects: cognitive, the affective and the conative. The cognitive aspect is responsible for our IQ or intellect. The affective comprises our emotional aspect. The conative aspect defines our desire to create and function. Our conative profile developed and defined within *The Conative Connection* by Kathy Kolbe* is responsible for our desire to create and move into action in the accomplishment of both major and minor tasks within human endeavor. (Page 119)

Creative/creation process: These two words are tied together to help explain the impact we make as individuals within humanity and how we are responsible for that which is created within the physical world. The most familiar activity we participate within through thoughts, words and deeds are those we can perceive through the five senses and what we define as creativity. Most important is that it should be understood that we play and share a more important role in the physical creation of our world within our conscious, subconscious and super-conscious mind activity. Our roles are integrated with the following groups of people: people who have lived, people who are living, and people who will live in the future. It should be understood that we are responsible for that which is made physical as a result of our individual and group desire patterns. It should be also understood that the physical world responds to these desire patterns and that it is within that creative/creation process that determines the world we build for ourselves. When one understands that we are responsible for that which exists, our ability to impact proactively that which will evolve within our physical world in the future will grow significantly.

Culture: Those ideas and perspectives gained through both formal and informal education. It is a result of how we have developed intellectually and morally over a lifetime that leads to behavior patterns. It is also a root cause leading to our ability to offer judgment of others as demonstrated and applied within the business environment. Culture can be considered a root cause of ethics in defining where business ethics begin. An example of a cultural statement within business was "let the buyer beware." This theory or reality will continue to fall by the wayside as business evolves in the direction of focusing on creating value to individuals.

Decision cycle: The process by which the conscious mind analyzes input from the five senses in order to respond to that environment with the proper emotional response tied to learned physical, mental, psychological, psychic and spiritual understanding/standards. The cycle happens either spontaneously or may happen over time as we analyze more complex situations such as in the business environment. The thought process within the cycle itself moves back and forth from positive to negative emotions until our assessment of the environment results in a reaction or decision to react.

Desire patterns: Everything that exists in this world on the physical, mental, emotional, psychological, psychic and above levels is the result or effect of individualized desire patterns. This desire to relate and experience by the superconscious mind or soul as defined within many spiritual and religious traditions is one of the most basic of root causes for what we experience within the world. These desire patterns at this point in time are considered to be uncontrollable. This is primarily due to the fact that the ego and conscious mind activity dominate our thoughts and vision and is where increasing awareness will impact that situation in the future.

Disparate parts: A summary of different ideas or concepts used to define business activities and areas within a company. They include such items as the company's marketing, financial and managements components (Pages 56 and 57) and activities that define how the company does business and how it creates value. An example of a disparate part within an organization would be a review of its product or service line features within its marketing mix that satisfy a base need or needs within its client groups. Does the way we deliver to our clients result in a transactional, tactical or strategic relationship with our clients which features the best balance for both our clients and ourselves? One of the most important responsibilities we have to our clients is to balance the disparate parts of our organizations environment in order to remain in business. (Page 1)

Ego (Ego sense): It is the common understanding and perspective that each of us is separate and distinct from each other. Feelings of separateness, due to our preoccupation in viewing this world from our conscious mind activity, is developed primarily through the five senses and is a result of our cognitive, affective and conative capabilities. It is this feeling of separateness that permits the mind to classify and judge other individuals and situations that lead to a breakdown in objectivity and discernment. This feeling of separateness is also a root cause of the tendency to feel competitive with each other within the business environment. (Page 20)

Egoic mind: Another term to describe the conscious mind activity as controlled by this idea of separateness. This egoic mind perspective diminishes in intensity through the awareness that separateness is a false perspective and is eliminated with understanding that we are all interconnected and impact each other's physical reality, both positively and negatively.

Ethics: The judgment, behavior and discipline dealing with a moral duty and obligation to each other or others within a group. Historically, they seek to structure that discussion and behavior into a right/wrong, legal/illegal, good/bad or honest/dishonest type perspective within the business arena. As leaders, a primary responsibility is to develop an environment where all people are placed in a position to function ethically at the highest levels. For us to do anything else is unethical. (Page 17)

Frame of reference: Our understanding and emotional response moment by moment to the understanding of immediate events observed through conscious and subconscious mind activity. How we judge the event is based on our individual standards and ethics concerning correct behavior. This frame of reference can change moment by moment as we gain more knowledge and information. This idea has been made popular within business circles by Stephen Covey. (Bibliography, page 205)

Hard dollars/soft dollars: These terms are used to describe quantitative and qualitative ideas of value. The term soft dollars include non-accounting and non-dollar type value and costs, such as opportunity cost, human capital investment and other expense and income ideas. Additional soft dollar issues and costs include relationship development cost and customer defection costs. In many cases, the historical focus has been on trying to convert soft dollar revenues and expenses into hard dollar measurements. Hard dollar costs include those found within generally accepted accounting principles where value is defined in terms of actual dollars within the major accounting statements such as the organizations balance sheet and income statement. (Page 3)

Knowing: Defined within the book as large K and small k knowing, I differentiate small k knowing as information gained from the conscious mind activity through the five senses. Large K knowing is driven by the development and expansion in our awareness that comes from the super-conscious mind activity. How we act reflects the type of knowledge, information and awareness within us and reveals itself through a person's behavior. It is a root cause leading to thoughts, words and deeds. (Page 30)

Knowledge network: It is the source from which we draw knowledge and insight from disparate parts of the physical environment and from individuals that influence our frame of reference and vision through their work and counsel. (Page 124)

Law of attraction: One of a number of natural laws that functions not only on the physical level, but on all levels within creation. It is suggested that for anything to manifest in the physical realm it must be attracted into a physical reality as a result of individual and/or group desire patterns and needs. This attracting process (an analogy can be equated to that of a magnet) is part of the super-conscious mind activity and is an important component or attribute of super-conscious mind. That which is required as output or value of the business process also finds itself operating within the law of attraction as a root cause for all business value that is created. Our ability to direct this attracting process is growing exponentially and will be a major root cause of the growth in business over the next 1,000 years. This concept has been developed and popularized within the works by Jerry and Ester Hicks (refer to Bibliography - page 205).

Mission statement: A statement of how the company creates value for the people it touches, from clients to employees, suppliers and shareholders. As the beginning part of defining the company's business model, it should be developed in such a way as to help give direction to all individuals touched by the organization from a value, creative and ethical perspective.

One hundred eighty (180) degree vision: As we expand our awareness into a broader understanding of our human condition, we find a change or evolution in our vision and reaction to all environmental factors as a leader. As stated in the Buddhist tradition in their attempt to explain behavior, our eight negative tendencies of the heart give way to positive tendencies or abilities of the heart. Our behavior and resulting insight also changes spontaneously and what we demonstrate in thought, word and deed reflects those of one who is said to be living free. They are involved in this world and business activity, but are not of it.

Out-of-body: Normally associated with an event (such as a near death or temporary death experience), the out of body experience would have the individual observe with conscious mind clarity the body and its environment from a point of view away from the physical body itself. The awareness that comes from that out-of-body event results in an understanding that our thoughts are not restricted to the physical body and that which is experienced after death is that which is being experienced now. Individuals experiencing the out of body situation come to an understanding that the mind can and does function beyond the confines of the physical body and in many cases, come to realize the physical body functions as a result of the mind activity, rather than the cause of that mind activity. Fear of death is also eliminated by the individual based on the intensity and clarity of the out of body experience.

Physicalization: The activity by which thoughts and vision become physical as a natural building block of this physical world. This would include how we are intimately involved in that which exists today through the creative/creation process that is constantly developing additional desire patterns. These developing desire patterns will be responsible for our future physical experience and existence. (Page 3)

Physicalization process: There are natural laws we utilize within our creative thought process that is a result of our desire patterns. These desire patterns are responsible for what is made physical through human endeavor and creativity. At this point in time business theory and principles are just beginning to discern these non-physical realities and will within the next 1,000 years come to be understood and used definitively in the creation of value.

Principles: Learned ideas, issues and methods of dealing with knowledge and information gained through formal and informal education. Principles within the business environment include accounting, finance, marketing and management related issues. The relationship between principles and ethics can be equated to the discussion concerning the chicken and the egg in order to answer which of the two came first. Principles and ethics do impact each other as part of the change that happens over time.

Problem chains: This term is used within the book to delineate a series of problems and solutions where one leads to the other in series, as well as cause and effect chains that lead to other causes and their effects. One of the examples in the book was the multiple cause and effect chain of events following the discovery of the western hemisphere 500 years ago. The need to constantly understand what precipitated the current situation and to focus on current decisions with an eye toward understanding objectively what future result those decisions will have is a skill that will develop significantly over the next millennium. From a vision perspective, this ability is especially important from a long term or strategic standpoint. This is especially true if the cause and effect chain leads to the proverbial blind alley. (Page 11)

Realization: We have the ability and capacity to know through conscious mind activity as insight or realization. Realization can be considered an event within the process of expanding awareness. This nonphysical event impacts our understanding of what is happening around us that leads to either a temporary or permanent change in our frame of reference. When the source of the idea or concept comes more directly from our super-conscious mind activity, its impact is more permanent and leads to a change in understanding and behavior without any need to condition or force that change. The positive tendencies of the heart spontane-ously arise within the conscious flow of thoughts and our behavior changes automatically. Increasing awareness does lead to heightened realizations and understanding. One of the ultimate results of realization is the individual func-tions in but not of the world. What this means is that the pain that comes within the normal human condition that is part of the ability to feel the eight negative tendencies or abilities of the heart is minimized or eliminated all together. That person is said to be in that state referred to as "living free."

Root cause: Everything that exists in this world on the physical, mental, emotional, psychological, psychic and above levels is the result or effect of "cause." In particular all that exists is at the end of extensively long cause and effect chains of ideas, events and activities. The idea of root cause suggests that as we follow these cause and effect chains back, we will eventually come to that cause which started the resulting chain. In many cases, especially within the problem solving mentality found today, that root cause is influencing more profoundly on the perceived problem than the problem itself. Both hierarchies and cycles, the two building type blocks of the physical world are con-structed from cause and effect chains of ideas and desire patterns each of us as individuals and groups create. These ideas and desire patterns drive purchasing and consumption behaviors in all of us. As an example, knowledge and information concerning the five cell functions within the individual cell and their impact on preserving and expanding the quality of physical life within the individual is a basic drive within self preservation. It should be understood to be a root cause of food consumption and should result in the food industry's focus, delivery and evolving structure. (Page 4)

Science: As used within the book, is a system of knowledge covering general truths or the operation of general laws responsible for what is created within the physical world that explain or provide the framework for creating something of value within business. This includes all bodies of knowledge, from manipulating the physical elements to create an object (e.g., understanding the process that turns petroleum into plastic to create a plastic writing stick — a pen) to understanding cell function and process to enhance the quality and longevity of life. (Page 40)

Service: The act of creating something of value to another individual or group that impacts them on either the physical, mental, emotional, psychological, psychic, spiritual levels and above. Most important within the book is an understanding of the hierarchy by which we go about creating something of value found within the personal service hierarchy and how the quality of life can be impacted positively by moving up that Service Hierarchy. (Page 40)

Soft dollars/ hard dollars: These terms are used to describe both accounting and dollar type expenses and non-accounting non-dollar type value and costs, such as opportunity cost, human capital investment and other non dollar expense ideas such as relationship and customer defection costs. Hard dollar costs include issues such as those found within generally acceptable accounting theory where value is defined in terms of actual dollars within the major accounting statements including balance sheet, income statement and cash flow summaries and include dollars received such as revenue and expense line items. (Page 3)

Spiritualism: As used within this book, an understanding and awareness of how we are all part of the creative/ creation process that is responsible for what materializes within this physical world. It is an understanding of how the idea of spirit from both a macro (religious) perspective and micro (individual) perspective is the root cause for all that exists and how business responds to that evolution in spirit by creating value. Also important is the evolving focus over the next 1,000 years in how business evolves its understanding of the creative/creation process minimizing unnecessary and wasted creative effort. This understanding will be as a result of the need to respond to the increased velocity of desire patterns. In the future, desire patterns will increase exponentially as evolving cycles and hierarchies of knowledge and information will grow. (Page 40)

Strategic management process: As used within this book, the process of focusing on disparate parts managed within all business entities either consciously or unconsciously. The process should seek to balance the focus within an organization's systems between issues related to marketing, accounting, financial and management activity, especially within the decision process and the focusing of participants' time and energy. When formalized, the process should both begin and include the point of difficulty clients have within their environment and basic needs concerning the type of products and services a company satisfies within the industry. An example of this is how an industry serves the desire patterns and physical reality (e.g., the point of difficulty clients have over time in managing their financial services needs and requirements) as tied to such ideas as their financial quality of life (i.e., Strategic Management Process Schematic located on pages 56 and 57 under physical environment. A Strategic Business Model would take their clients over time from a 96/4 situation to a 4/40 environment.)

Strategy: As used within the book, it is both a broad or macro idea of how a company creates value within its business and industry as well as numerous micro ideas, words and activities that individuals use to both understand and deliver that which they do to create value for their clients, be they internal (company) individuals or external (customers, suppliers and shareholders) individuals and groups. (Page 50)

Super-conscious mind: The term is used within the book to describe at the highest level of mind activity that aspect that controls issues of life within the individual and which has access to all knowledge and information. Within all world religions, the concept of super-conscious mind is referred to as soul, spirit, or individualized spirit. Its attributes includes participating on all ongoing activity of individual experiences on all levels including the physical, mental, emotional, psychological, psychic and spiritual levels. Additional levels within the hierarchy of mind activity are referred to as conscious and subconscious mind activity. (Page 34)

Ten second test: A test to demonstrate two ideas leading to expanded awareness: (1) We can observe the conscious mind and its thoughts as an observer that lead to the ability to detach from those thoughts. (2) We are not in control of future thoughts and creativity on a moment to moment basis within the conscious mind activity. (Page 5)

Two-dimensional (perspective) thinking: As used within the book, it is the natural conscious mind process that looks and assesses that which is being observed through the five senses and then ranks what is seen within the cognitive (I.Q.), affective (emotional) and conative (desire) areas of the brain. This two-dimensional thinking leads to judging activity within the physical world as right/wrong, good/evil, moral/immoral, ethical/unethical and as such responds with a problem-solving mindset found prevalent today within leadership and business theory and practice. It is also this two dimensional mindset that moves the individual to be consumed with proving the rightness of his or her perspective in the desire to fashion his or her endeavors into a competitive environment. (Pages 21, 46, and 48)

Value: As used throughout the book, it is the idea or physical object or service individuals and groups seek in order to satisfy conscious, subconscious or super-conscious desire patterns. Creation of value is at the center of why a business entity exists. Normally equated with a dollar equivalent or concept, value is a multidimensional concept that increases the quality of life and/or satisfies a need within our individual hierarchy of needs as articulated within Abraham H. Maslow's "Hierarchy of Needs" that range from physiological and physical needs including food, water and shelter to self actualized needs of acceptance and self worth. It is our ability to see and deliver value within a business entity that is responsible for a business transaction between a buyer and seller. (Page 1)

Vision: As used within the book, it is the ability to discern or understand through awareness that which is both physical and nonphysical in nature. It is the ability to see (not associated with sight as in one of the five senses within the human body) with the conscious mind. An example within the leadership of a business entity would be an understanding of how to create and share value through organizing and directing activity that results in an ever growing quality of life for all participants over an extended period of time. (Page 19). It is from vision that an ethical environment is created by leaders.

Appendix

A

Case Study

CASE STUDY:
Financial Services/Banking Industry

Change can move a business environment in both positive and negative directions, and it is its inherent risk that can make it a feared activity. When 180-degree vision is lacking (as discussed within the book), we can as participants be unaware of what we are a part. What decisions are made over time may in turn be less than ethical in nature.

The following case addresses part of what has happened within the banking and financial services industry over the last 30 years and serves as an example of how well-intentioned and ethical people can ultimately falter.

In the instance of the deregulation each of us who participated within the financial industry (from elected legislative and government administrators, to financial services leaders, executives, managers and employees) became part of creating a more difficult and perplexing environment for all concerned, from our customers to our employees and shareholders.

Prior to 1980, the commercial banking and savings and loan industry was regulated and kept separated from the insurance industry and equity/stock market industry. This separation dated back to the early 20th century with regulations such as the McFadden Act of 1927, and the Glass-Steagall Act of 1933.

Within the banking industry, companies were regulated as to where they could operate geographically as well as to what products and services they could offer and at what price. Most components within the marketing mix (pages 56 and 57) were set and standard.

Within this very important industry, financial standards within many of the components described on pages 56 and 57 became ones by which companies were judged as "well run." Two efficiency ratios accepted as important industry measures were the return on assets (ROA) and return on equity (ROE) of the company or bank. These benchmarks are illustrated as a subcomponent within the section exploring financial principles and process (box labeled "net income") on pages 56 and 57. Prior to 1980, the ROA statistic suggested that a well run banking company should earn from point eight (.8) percent to one (1.0) percent return on its assets (i.e., a one billion dollar bank should earn 8 to 10 million dollars as net income after taxes). A major reason for that accepted standard was that regulation of banks and savings and loans defined how much they could

pay in interest and charge for loans, as government standards restricted maximum interest rates.

Beginning in 1980 and lasting for more than 15 years,
the deregulation of interest rates, restriction of geographic
locations where companies could operate, combined with
past regulations that prevented certain financial institutions
(banks, insurance companies, and brokerage firms) from
offering certain products and services restrictions were all
but eliminated. The marketing mix components stated on
pages 56 and 57 were no longer standard and as such, the
leadership of banks was faced with new and constantly
changing situations.

Growth of an improper industry standard over time

The previously described situation led to a redefining of
performance including the return on assets (ROA) statistic.
Due to inflation during the late 1970s and early 1980s, as
well as deregulated interest rates (where mortgage rates
reached a high of 15 to 20 percent and certificate of deposit
rates hit levels up to 15 percent), the new level of the ROA
statistic moved to a 1.5 percent return on the assets of a
bank from 1.0 percent as a target high performance rate (a
bank with one billion dollars in assets should now earn 15
million dollars, or five to seven million dollars more each
year).

At that time, the 50 percent increase in this new target
rate was considered fair, as one of the measures of what
was fair and ethical in the process of creating and sharing
value (among customers, employees, suppliers and shareholders) as interest rates rose during that post-regulation
era.

During that time an additional statistic that drove the definition of high performance was the return on equity (ROE). This statistic was used along with the focus on the management of assets (loans and investments) and liabilities (deposits) and their relationship to the net interest margin (the size and spreads between assets and liabilities) that began to drive profitability models used to manage profitability, set interest rates for loans and deposits that were now changing daily, and specify the level of income desired. The deregulation of interest rates alone significantly heightened the point of difficulty on what was required to manage a bank in a deregulated interest rate environment.

It was also the overnight deregulation of interest rates that resulted in the savings and loan associations having deposits that now cost an average of more than 10 percent as an expense, and 30-year mortgage loans made prior to deregulation that yielded a 6.50 to 8.50 percent income level — well below what they now had to pay for deposits to fund the loans as money immediately flowed into the higher priced certificates of deposits.

(Author's note) Improper industry standard: An improper industry standard is one that leads to creating an unethical environment for people touched by the company's activity by creating an imbalance in the creating and sharing of value between clients, employees, suppliers and shareholders.

In this case study, the standard led to profitability models that drove the development and elimination of product/ loan categories and the drive to obtain higher yielding loans and investments such as mortgage back securities and other off-balance sheet type activity.

A root cause of the consolidating process: What created the consolidating process for 25 years that is now being experienced within the industry due to the 1.5 percent standard was the interest rate environment that began to **fluctuate** because of the deregulation of interest rates and competition. During that same period, the 1.5 percent standard became **fixed** in nature as a measure of how well a company was performing. This 1.5 percent standard was also used to determine how well the company was being managed when compared to other firms within the industry and drove both the long and short-term financial management process. The 1.5 percent standard helped evolve leadership principles and practices deemed appropriate in order to realize high performance status within the financial service community and the investment community in general. For those individuals who wish to create a competitive environment in which to function professionally, the financial industry provided that circumstance. The balance between a service perspective and competitive perspective was lost, especially within the financial management of the industry companies.

Author's note: *As the book addresses, all of this physical reality is subjected to cycles and hierarchies as a root cause of what we experience. In the case of general interest rates and their fluctuating nature within a competitive environment, these interest rate levels soon experienced a long-term sustained drop and today are one-tenth to one-third their original highs.*

The financial management of each individual company, through normal budgeting and financial planning processes, resulted in an imbalance of priorities with a **fixed** profitability standard and a major **fluctuating** interest rate income and expense environment.

Managing straight line growth in income and profitability became a precursor to determining what activities within the areas of product and service enhancements were entertained creatively, and determined how these enhancements added quickly to the bottom line. Earnings that did not dillute short term shareholder value became most important in everything from loans, deposit and service areas, to acquisitions and how they were justified and structured.

As industry participants focused more on meeting fixed financial standards of performance, the demands placed on those responsible became more intense. A long held objective of creating knowledgeable long-term clients, employees, suppliers and shareholders gave way to an environment that discounted their importance. That which replaced the leadership standard focused on short term hard dollar reprising, expense control and other tactical approaches of hitting the profitability targets that included the 1.5 ROA. Nothing was designed to lead to increasing the ability of participants to act in a highly ethical manner. This lead to trends that generated shorter-term customers, employees and shareholder relationships overtime.

From out-sourcing of activity and staff to the continuous downsizing and consolidation of staff, an industry known for individuals that worked entire careers at one organization began to fall by the wayside.

So what happened to the industry's customers and clients during this period, as well as its employees?

The deregulation of interest rates and industry restrictions eliminated the **safety net** that provided people with a safe haven for their money and assured its ability to earn a consistent rate of return. For those employed within the industry, the point of difficulty of leading a deregulated company has expanded exponentially; subjecting these companies to an environment that demonstrates significantly higher levels of risk to everyone it touches over time, from customers and employees to shareholder and suppliers – truly an unethical environment in which to spend one's time.

How does an organization or industry deal with an improper standard that has generated a difficult and unethical environment for clients, employees, shareholders and suppliers?

The answer is to change that standard to a new standard that helps balance specific strategic components (pages 56 and 57).

In the case of the ROA statistic, 180-degree vision suggests that it is realistic to change that ratio to a range between .50 percent on assets to a high of 1.0 percent on assets (in the case of the one billion dollar bank, a net income level of five to ten million dollars as opposed to fifteen million per year) would reflect a more balanced level of appreciating value to shareholders while fulfilling the requirement to fund growing market and human capital needs as well as staying competitively priced with other companies.

Therefore, the lower return would reflect a more even balance in the level of value sharing (especially at the current level of interest rates), where decisions can reflect the importance of human capital, practical experience, and the knowledge and information that comes with creating a more appropriate product and service for clients as their basic needs continue to expand.

It would help create an environment where business models move from what can be considered a fear-based model or competitive business model to one that focuses on developing and simplifying increased information and knowledge for both business and personal clients. This strategic type business model begins the process of developing need-based knowledge and information to increase a client's quality of life through the managing of their financial needs and requirements. It could be a business model that would help clients gain and maintain their financial independence.

(Author's Note) Question: From our understanding of our role as leaders, in addition to restructuring our profitability standards, what other issues (pages 56 and 57) should we focus on to create a more ethical financial services environment for everyone concerned? What goals or mission would we want to accomplish?

Appendix

B

**Quick Reference Guide:
Chapters**

*Definitions, page 167

**Bibliography, page 193

***Root ideas, page 144

Chapter One includes a brief introduction and summary of important ideas and trends. The book is written with ideas that should be contemplated over time based on the needs of the reader. Summaries have been added to the end of each chapter that come to conclusions or restates some of the major ideas found within the chapter. For instance, if one finds himself or herself with the task of revisiting his or her company's strategy, he or she might want to revisit Chapter Two because it addresses integrating the Four Ss to start the "back to basics" type discussion that should be the starting point of any effective strategic or operational planning process.

Chapter Two addresses the Four Ss both in defining a more comprehensive definition of these concepts and how they are responsible for the increased velocity of change*. The focus on leadership over the next one thousand years will include the impact these four areas will have on increasing the quality of life within the human condition.

Chapter Three summarizes a new definition of strategic management from a 180-degree perspective for defining a company's mission statement and resulting business model*. This chapter presents a new millennium focus within the strategic management process.

I have used the analogy that without 180-degree vision, current leadership activity can be equated to sitting on the bank of the river and paddling to help the water continue flowing downstream, and taking credit for its downstream flow. Without 180-degree vision, a leader increases the probability that he or she will focus individuals on activities that may not add value or on risks that may not exist.

Chapter Three also suggests that the organization complete a 180-degree turnaround within its method of managing disparate strategic components (strategic management process, pages 56 and 57). These strategic components are part of the business's internal and external environment and should be treated with less permanence. This is because of the increased velocity of change happening today. It is also due to the point of difficulty in maintaining balance within these changing components.

The increased velocity of change is due primarily to the evolving desire patterns of individuals. These evolving desire patterns are a result of the expansion in knowledge and information. This expansion leads to an impact on awareness concerning the Four Ss, including strategy*, science*, spirituality* and service* and further change in buying patterns.

The chapter also deals with a new way of looking at the role of business in general and your role in particular. It discusses how awareness of extreme opposites presents choices that we normally do not know exist. This is especially true if one is trying to define a new personal ethic that helps discern when systems and policies are moving in the right direction.

Chapter Four starts to define a new leadership perspective by presenting a personal service hierarchy (page 91) for the business leader. If you are like most people, your current perspective has evolved significantly since you started your career. The chapter contains a discussion on the root causes of ethics, standards and how the ego* must be minimized in order for a higher level of 180-degree thinking to develop effortlessly.

Chapter Five presents a leadership hierarchy (page 100) that helps the reader analyze where they could be within their decision cycle and motivation. This chapter covers an important process, for the future leader must be able to develop a skill set that contains the process of observing the conscious mind's flow of thoughts. It is objectivity and awareness that results in the development of an environment that enhances the creation/creative process. This enhanced creation/creative process culminates in exponential growth in all aspects of performance and value created.

Chapter Six shows the areas impacted due to our decisions and level of awareness of these choices we make as leaders and business participants. The management hierarchy (page 117) helps demonstrate how current leadership principles have not gone far enough in defining the multiple directions our roles are as problem solvers and motivators. The hierarchy suggests something more than two-dimensional thinking as part of the conscious mind activity that defines our environment in terms of right and wrong or good and bad. This is found within the problem-solving activity we were taught within our formal business school education when a definition and standard was developed in defining our roles as leaders. These standards included a process that defines our environment as external and internal risks or factors to focus on and solve, but can also result in the attraction of these issues into our acceptance as real.

Chapter Seven covers the "now what?" question that will arise as we are moved to go forward in a proactive way to enhance our quality of life and the people we touch.

The very personal growth process I address in this book is shared through a list of individuals that can help direct you to sources of information. I have found that these sources will stimulate a change within a person's frame of reference. This is especially true in the expansion and integration of the Four Ss. The list includes sources I have discovered in broadening my vision over the last 35 years as I have seen business theory and practice develop.

Chapter Eight is a Student Supplemental Summary that helps explain the situation students experience within both the formal and informal learning environment, and how they create their own ethical perspective by understanding the importance they will play in the future of leadership and ethics.

Appendix

C

Discussion Points
from Chapter 2

*Definitions, page 167

**Bibliography, page 193

***Root ideas, page 144

Discussion point:

evolving business perspectives; evolving standards

A more general example of how business theory, focus and awareness was impacted by a new standard of looking at business and its evolution can be demonstrated by the work of John Naisbitt ** as stated in his book *Megatrends*, that the leading industrial countries had changed from being manufacturing to information-based societies. It should be understood today that recent upheavals in the business sector are giving way to a new era in business and its focus within value creation.

Naisbitt defined this change as a physical change in the number of jobs held by people doing non-manufacturing tasks. It was determined that over 50 percent of workers fell into this non-manufacturing category.

It should be understood that the increase in the rate of change of what people use is also giving way to a new era in business and its focus within value creation. I believe a new culture is evolving that will continue to focus on information, but will also be concerned with the process by which something becomes physical as a value-creating activity. It will include society's move to a new level of understanding to how best be part of what becomes physical in the future and how we participate from a proactive rather than reactive role.

For example, the reactive role today reflects an orientation that finds comfort with past precedence rather than enhancing clear understanding of evolving desire patterns. This will give way to a more realistic perspective concerning how risks associated with the physicalization of both product and services can be minimized.

So based on what Naisbitt presented 25 years ago, what will be the next great breakthrough in business and social theory?

What major change or evolution is occurring right now?

I suggest that the information society is giving way to an awareness society. The core of this change is understanding how we are proactive in our world. Through our abilities we are responsible for what is happening around us. By understanding that we are not passive observers but are responsible for the results that are created, we can enhance our creative capability that results in the physicalization of ideas and an expansion in the quality of the life for ourselves and others.

This book is also about understanding how we go about creating the physicalization of desire patterns. An example within the personal data processing industry is the personal computer, which can be considered the first practical tool that expands our mental capabilities. The desire by those that use them permits them to handle more information many times faster and more efficiently. This basic need to know and handle more knowledge and information within all of us is a primary reason for its success, a story in and of itself.

I also suggest that if we are to be part of the leadership evolution over the next 1,000 years, an evolving skill set will develop that is driven by a person's ability to impact and expand awareness of this physical world. Leaders will understand and take objective responsibility for the creation process in which we are all involved.

Discussion point:

extended Chapter Two summary

The ability to see that this entire physical world is made up of hierarchies and cycles (from the grandest to the most minute) on a number of different levels, will be all important. Increased focus on knowledge and information about the workings and diversity of these hierarchies and cycles will be required by those who both lead and follow. How these hierarchies and cycles perpetuate themselves on physical, mental, emotional, psychological, psychic, and spiritual levels will help lead to insight that will permit the leader to grow, shrink, modify, end or sustain these constantly changing processes. It will lead to an understanding of the root causes of those aspects of our physical existence that are responsible for the need to create. The issues will be as basic as an understanding of the creative or creation process that leads to desire patterns, which in turn lead to those concepts we have defined as wants and needs of clients within the business arena.

Large "K" knowledge and understanding of the infinite series of cause and effect chains of what we experience with our conscious mind and five senses will require a focus on a comprehensive understanding of how strategy, science, spirituality and service are integrated to form behavior — behavior that drives everything from purchasing decisions to how all groups form conscious and subconscious wants and needs.

A focus that results from understanding an expanded definition of each of the Four Ss will be needed to comprehend the diversity of attitudes and behavior within those groups that move them to action. This expanding awareness of the importance of our conscious and super-conscious mind process should have a direct impact on our decisions and actions and should help change our preoccupation with what we believe or judge to be correct at any point in time to that which will direct our energy towards enhanced perceptions of our constituents, including shareholders, employees, customers and potential customers concerning their current and evolving desire patterns.

The knowledge and information we receive and act upon is a function of what we do or do not see, as well as what we believe (spiritually believe and understand concerning the physicalization process). As leaders, we are constantly asked to deal with the physical environment based on our understanding of how it manifests value. We are commanded to be seers and guarantee a future result.

As with the example used in the book concerning the discovery of the Western Hemisphere 500 years ago and the eventual creation of the wealthiest country in the world, all four Ss were impacted with that one piece of awareness or information that addresses a change in awareness and which overcomes the prevailing belief system. In the previously mentioned scenario that the world is round and not flat, a religious* doctrine had suggested that there were evil forces awaiting those who tried to defy the old belief system and that dissenters could expect to die by falling off the edge of the world.

When one looks at the point of difficulty in creating value today, as defined by future behavior, changing needs and attitudes and our requirement to eliminate risk and communicate our personal responsibility to an absolute result, it is no wonder that we are likely focused on the wrong things with the wrong information, driven by bad or false information with ulterior motives. We are forced by the threat of being ostracized to validate that perception that we are visionaries (of a future effect) with an ability to guarantee results with a very high degree of probability (it is here that truth takes on a life of its own, or lack thereof). In other words, we risk dying a thousand deaths in principles, emotion, mental anguish, and failure. All of the above begs the question, "Is this not the physical world we are asked to participate within as business participants?"

And in turn, aren't we asked to set a standard that deals with the issue of "ethics" within it, where ethics are talked about as an absolute in their provincial two-dimensional definition?

So how does a person (who finds himself or herself in the above situation) increase the quality of his or her life? By expanding our frame of reference through awareness of what is responsible for what drives the physical or material realm and to tie into the creative consciousness that is responsible for its manifestation, we may choose not to be of it but function within it.

Bibliography

—

Webography

Cayce, Edgar. **The Essential Edgar Cayce**. Mark Thurston, PhD, editor. New York: Tarchen/Penguin, 2004. www.penguin.com.

Chodron, Pema. **Awakening Loving-Kindness**. Boston: Random House, 1991. www.shambhala.com.

Chopra, Deepak. **The Seven Spiritual Laws of Success: A Practical Guide to the Fulfillment of Your Dreams**. Amber-Allen Publishing. www.deepakchopra.com.

Covey, Stephan R. **Principle Centered Leadership**. New York: Free P, 1992. www.franklincovey.com.

Covey, Stephan R. **The 7 Habits of Highly Effective People**. New York: Free P, 1990. www.franklincovey.com.

Davis, Roy E. **Master Guide to Meditation and Spiritual Growth**. N.p. : Motilal Banarsidass, 1997. www.csa-davis.org.

Davis, Roy E. **The Path of Light**. N.p. : Motilal Banarsidass, 2002. www.csa-davis.org.

De Mello, Anthony. **Awareness**. New York: Doubleday, 1990. www.amazon.com.

Hicks, Esther and Jerry. **Ask and it Is Given**. Abraham-Hicks Publication. www.abraham-hicks.com.

Kolbe, Kathy. **Conative Connection**. Canada: Addison-Wesley, 1990. www.kolbe.com.

Maslow, Abraham H. **Maslow on Management**. Canada: John Wiley & Sons, Inc. 1998. www.maslow.com.

Pearce, Terry, and David S. Pottruck. **Clicks and Mortar**. San Francisco: Jossey-Bass, 2001. www.terrypearce.com.

Peters, Thomas. **In Search of Excellence: Lessons from America's Best Run Companies**. New York: Warner Books, 1988. www.tompeters.com.

Peters, Thomas. **The Pursuit of Wow**. New York: Vintage Books, 1994. www.tompeters.com

Ruiz, Don Miguel. **The Four Agreements**. Amber-Allen Publishing. www.amazon.com.

Tolle, Eckart. **The Power of Now: A Guide to Spiritual Enlightenment**. Novato: New World Library, 1999. www.amazon.com.

Weil, Andrew, M.D. **Healthy Aging**. New York: Random-House, Inc., 2005. www.drweil.com.

Yogananda, Paramahansa. **Autobiography of a Yogi**. Los Angeles: Self Realization Fellowship, 1946. www.selfrealizationfellowship.com.

Yuen, Dr. Kam. **Instant Healing**. www.yuenmethod.com.

Acknowledgments

May I start by acknowledging all who have lived, are living now, and who will live in the future? Those who have lived are responsible for the hierarchies in knowledge and information existing to date. For those who are living, it is their responsibly to expand on these hierarchies or building blocks within this physical world. And for those who will live, I hope you realize what has been created for you and will reap the benefits of our energy and focus within business today.

Having said that, my eldest daughter Jeanne suggested with her publicist background that I might want to narrow the above down, so may I give my heartfelt appreciation to those who have touched me directly.

To my new wife and mate, Lynette, for showing such patience and understanding with the twists and turns I have been able to provide. I also appreciate her direct work in simplifying the message as I tried to expand and develop the information into a more "how to" approach in the development of this edition.

To my three children for their strength and understanding of the major life events we have shared, including the death of my late wife and their mother, Barbara.

To my son, Tom, for taking that experience and focusing on the health and skin care industry and the role it will have in extending and expanding the quality of life we live.

To my older daughter, Jeanne, for writing and letting me know that what I was trying to accomplish was worth something, at a time when I needed it, and in applying her formal communication education to look over the work and give support.

To my younger daughter, Julie, for helping me to round out my fathering skills that led to a greater insight into our roles beyond our sometimes very narrow business careers.

To my many family members, including my father as he reached 90 years of age and continues to be involved with life. And my mother, for teaching me to always question those who would make standards and rules for others and who had a true thirst for the knowledge of life.

To my five brothers and sisters (Maureen, Bill, Teri, Marty and John) for being the toughest of teachers, as only siblings can be. And for that special mate of my eldest brother, Bill, who has been the kindest of teachers.

To Jody, my editor, and David, my publishing consultant and facilitator from Serey/Jones, for taking their combined experience of more than 50 years and applying it to what they called a worthwhile endeavor. To Caryn for introducing me to Jody following our chance meeting and conversation flying over the high desert country of the Southwest.

To so many business professionals that have provided me with a career long learning environment, from my graduate level professor, Dr. McNamara, who was able to teach me marketing with the passion and love very few had demonstrated, even after a full career as a business professional, including the role of President of M&M Mars.

To all my past managers and bosses including Walt, who helped me as a young teenager to develop a strong work ethic. To Bruce and Howard who gave me a chance to get involved in banking and the start to my second career goal (to be part of an organization interested in redefining the delivery of services to clients within that industry). To Grace G. who placed me in a position to round out my business education by teaching what I had learned. To Fletcher, Ash, Tom, Everet, Don, Frank and finally John and Tom. Although all were bosses and mangers, I count at least one of them as a most powerful teacher and a few as close friends. All of them showed me how great leaders can be when they are thinking right, to how brutal they can be when thinking wrong. All demonstrated behavior within the natural cycles we are all susceptible to when offering up judgment. Judgment that is also part of the natural cycles of positive and negative emotion and frame of reference within the natural human condition addressed within this book.

To fellow employees and suppliers who have worked with me and against me as peers and friends, whether they realized it or not, which helped me develop my own creative leadership model in trying to impact and change their individual frames of reference. Especially those that have been there over the length of my entire financial services and marketing career, including Jack who helped move the banking industry into its relationship focus, and Al, Jim and Bill who represents true business banker's.

To other bank marketing professionals including Mike, Don, Pat, Olga, Jim, and Judy. To Lew who has became a close friend and counsel for the last 25 years on many comprehensive business issues from leadership to research — a true entrepreneur.

To those individuals who have worked with me and for me, which was always one and the same within my management style and which help me develop my own leadership skills. To Rita, Sharon, Michelle, Floyd, Betty, Renee, Judy, Mike, Tom (who became the closest of family friends), Shirley, Nona, Kay (the sweetest and nicest of ladies) and Laurie who all spent many years with me within the different positions and activities performed.

To Brian and Bren for providing me with fresh eyes to try and simplify and move this edition into a more how to approach.

To those leadership gurus that I mention at different times throughout this book and in chapter seven as the best source for knowledge and information that will expand the reader's frame of reference and awareness.

And finally, to those individuals participating in everything from the entertainment industry to medical professionals and healers that demonstrate the power of love and empathy. Especially to that television personality that to the author demonstrates how powerful that medium can be in impacting positively on the quality of life.

www.ingramcontent.com/pod-product-compliance
Lightning Source LLC
Chambersburg PA
CBHW021557210326
41599CB00010B/490